"What a gift for anyone navigating or considering navigating the world of scale-ups! A witty, thoughtful and highly pragmatic handbook for evaluating if scale-ups are the place for you, and how to mea… ngfully look under the hood to interrogate the bluster, deeply consi… k/reward, chaos/fun, youth/experience trade-offs in scale-… ished players. It also offers guidance on how to tack… metimes messy but often very rewarding wo…

What I especially lov… ursting with frameworks, thought-p… opportunities for reflection and pra… essential for success in scale-up land, a… this space."

…, *Commercial, Skyscanner*

"Many people feel they can be successful in scale-ups simply by being smart and having a good track record in other environments. They are often caught by surprise – only to quit or burn out. This book provides the much-needed toolkit to navigate the challenges of working in a scale-up.

I found the insights valuable – not just reflecting on my own behaviour but also in better understanding the behaviour of others. The frameworks and case studies bring lessons vividly to life. Think of this as an equivalent of several hours of mentoring and coaching from successful scale-up leaders. This is a must-read for anyone transitioning to a scale-up business, or already working in one but struggling with its challenges."

Dan Warne, *CEO at Sessions;*
former managing director, Deliveroo

"This book is a must-read for any professional pondering entry into – or already navigating the scale-up world. Vidya has encapsulated a wealth of wisdom and insight in an engaging and approachable style, enabling a wide spectrum of professionals to benefit. These experiences are impactfully wrapped in a narrative that is educational and honest, consistently offering the reader with opportunities to reflect and. I am sure I won't be the only one thinking, 'I wish I had this book 20 years ago,' as I firmly believe I would have approached a number of situations more effectively with this context as a guide."

Carmen Carey, *experienced CEO/COO for tech*
scale-up businesses across the US and EU

How to Survive in a Scale-Up Business

Working in a scale-up is exciting, but it can also be exhausting. This book is your emotional survival kit for succeeding in a fast-paced and unpredictable environment.

Scale-ups attract ambitious, driven and hardworking individuals seeking excitement, ownership, freedom and greater rewards. However, these opportunities often come with challenges. Understanding the emotional and behavioural patterns commonly seen in scale-ups – and learning from others' experiences – can help you move from struggling to thriving.

In this book, author Vidya Murali brings together:

- A personal scale-up suitability checklist to help assess and understand whether scale-ups are the right environment for you based on your skills and preferences.
- Guidance on what to look for when interviewing, and how to set yourself up for success in the first 90 days.
- Insights, frameworks and coaching questions to tackle toxic patterns commonly seen in scale-ups.
- Real-life case studies from scale-up leaders with lessons and strategies.
- Practical strategies for introverts, highly sensitive people, ethnic minorities and people with ADHD and/or dyslexia to thrive in scale-ups.
- Tools for building your emotional skills to progress and thrive in scale-ups – including if you lose your job or face a mental health breakdown.

A must-read for anyone transitioning into scale-ups or already working in one, this book will be of immense interest to graduates seeking their first full-time role, professionals transitioning from corporate environment, leaders – including founders – as well as HR professionals and coaches.

Vidya Murali has been working in the UK's leading tech businesses, including Amazon, and high-growth scale-ups such as Deliveroo. Having grown up in India before moving to the UK in 2006 and completing her MBA at the University of Cambridge, Vidya brings a unique perspective as a woman of colour and an introvert navigating high-growth and fast-paced business environments. She experienced significant anxiety in the wake of the pandemic, which prompted her to reflect on what matters most and prioritise her well-being. During this time, she started practising mindfulness meditation and began supporting others through coaching and mentoring.

She now holds a leadership position and supports her colleagues and clients as they navigate the exciting – yet chaotic – environment of fast-moving scale-ups, helping them navigate the challenges and seize opportunities and thrive.

How to Survive in a Scale-Up Business

Master the Human Skills Needed to Thrive in Young, High-Growth Businesses

Vidya Murali

Routledge
Taylor & Francis Group
NEW YORK AND LONDON

Designed cover image: Getty Images

First published 2026
by Routledge
605 Third Avenue, New York, NY 10158

and by Routledge
4 Park Square, Milton Park, Abingdon, Oxon OX14 4RN

Routledge is an imprint of the Taylor & Francis Group, an informa business

British Library Cataloguing-in-Publication Data
A catalogue record for this book is available from the British Library

ISBN: 978-1-032-93370-2 (hbk)
ISBN: 978-1-032-91186-1 (pbk)
ISBN: 978-1-003-56559-8 (ebk)

DOI: 10.4324/9781003565598

Typeset in Sabon
by KnowledgeWorks Global Ltd.

Dedicated to our human qualities – curiosity, compassion and connection, and our intention to thrive individually and as a collective!

Contents

Acknowledgements

The idea of writing this book came about during a casual conversation with a colleague who was asking for coaching for her husband after he had joined a scale-up and found it tricky to work with his founder. I, jokingly, remarked, "I have had so many weird and wonderful experiences in scale-ups, I can actually write a book." My wise colleague responded with sincerity, "That sounds like a great idea! Why don't you?" That chat then led to a series of LinkedIn posts and got me thinking about why this book matters. So, thank you to my colleague and friend for that timely prompt.

My heartfelt gratitude to my hardworking and committed parents who invested in my education back in India, stretching beyond their financial means at times. They also instilled in me the ability to challenge accepted social norms and protected my ability to think independently. Thanks to my brother, grandparents, aunt, uncle and my cousins, whom I lived with in my formative years, for building my confidence as well as giving me such varied experiences, and to all my extended family for your encouragement till date. A special call out to my late paternal grandfather, who instilled self-esteem and integrity in me, by living these values in the most challenging of times. Thanks to Naveen for the support with the manuscript preparation.

A big thank you to my husband Kamesh and daughter Shakthi, who have supported me and put up with me sitting in front of my laptop for hours during the weekends, and our adorable dog baby Simba who had cuddled by my side while I wrote.

Thank you to my interviewees for their time and honest contributions, which have made this book relatable and insightful to the readers. I, obviously, am not naming them for anonymity reasons. You are all amazing!

Thanks to my beta readers and endorsers who have spent hours reading my first manuscripts and helped shape the book to this version. Your time and generosity are much appreciated.

To my wellbeing support team-mindfulness teacher, mentors, fitness instructors and, doctors who have all helped me stay my best self during this time.

To all my friends and colleagues who have encouraged, challenged and, supported me through this journey, thank you!

To Alison, who helped me understand the process of writing a book, thank you!

Finally, a big thank you to my editor, Meredith Norwich, copyeditor and, publisher, for choosing my work and taking it to this point, without whom this book would have been the world's best-kept secret. I hope that as an underrepresented woman of colour author, this book will inspire my fellow women of colour to publish.

This book is a result of a fantastic teamwork!

To all you readers who have chosen to pick this book in this content-loaded world, thank you for trusting me with your time!

Part I

Introduction

Chapter 1

Why I wrote this book

I believe that every suffering is transformational, not just for the individual but the wider community. If this is intriguing for you, I hope you will understand the profoundness of this statement as you read the book.

It was a cold November day when I met my coachee, Karthik,[1] in a dimly lit central London coffee shop. Something was not quite right with Karthik on that day. He appeared restless, and as we sat down with our coffees, he started speaking, "I have been unable to focus on anything outside my work. I feel let down by my founders. I know this is not something I should worry about, but I can't take my mind off it. What happened is not logical. Why?" Karthik felt stuck and unable to decide what he needed to do next and how to make sense of the situation. Karthik, eventually, decided to resign and move on, as he had lost his respect and trust for the founders.

In the months before this meeting, Karthik's manager had resigned, and he had taken on more responsibilities with the promise of a promotion. Karthik gave all he could and exerted himself in this process, only to realise later that the founders had been interviewing to replace his ex-manager's role behind his back. When Karthik travelled to meet the founders at the headquarters, expecting his promotion to be formally announced, he was informed that someone was joining as his manager. He was shocked and desperate to understand why things turned out this way. That's when he called me to chat.

The situation like the one Karthik faced are more common than you might think in scale-ups. Many feel they have the expertise and skills to succeed in scale-ups. Yet, they struggle to succeed and thrive, eventually leading to burnout and/or quitting the business!

My experience was no different in that aspect but very different in many others. In my twenties, I moved countries (from India to the UK), pursued an MBA at the University of Cambridge, joined a big tech company and then transitioned to scale-ups after six years. Little did I know about the roller coaster ride ahead of me! If I were to choose a persona for a big tech company, it would be that of a parent – the kind of parent who raises a top

DOI: 10.4324/9781003565598-2

athlete. The parent who set clear rules and boundaries, provided resources and knowledge to help you perform and kept challenging and pushing, while most scale-ups are like teenagers, who want to conquer the world and operate with unclear rules, if any, no boundaries and very limited resources, and as far as knowledge, well that was supposed to come from you! The need for growth is greater, and they push you much harder. Being a mum of one right now, I get it in hindsight:). No one told me how different it is going to be before I took the plunge to join scale-ups, and I was both surprised by the fun dynamism and shocked by the lack of maturity I experienced. What shocked me most was trying to find logic in people's behaviour—logic that simply didn't exist, unlike in the structured world of big business. It's funny to think about it now, but it was not the case then. This is the book I wish I had read a decade back when I made that move quite so naively, assuming my skills, smarts, logic and experience alone would suffice to succeed in scale-ups.

> Most of the time, the shock was trying to determine the rationale behind people's behaviours when they were none, something I took for granted in successful big businesses.

I first joined a scale-up because I wanted to make an impact. I was tired of being a small fish in a big pond, regularly writing several versions of documents to update my work and constantly having to prove my knowledge in big meetings. Scale-ups sounded like the welcome relief I needed, where I could make a tangible impact and enjoy a flexible, no-fuss culture. Well, my wishes came true, but at a cost. I enjoyed the dynamic, passionate, no-fuss and growth culture, but dealing with inexperienced leaders, scope changes, ambiguity, uncertainty and confusion with little guidance was painful.

As a woman of colour, introvert and working mother, I experienced unique challenges in terms of integrating with the team. Then COVID hit, and at the same time, I experienced significant anxiety. My suffering led to personal growth. I set out to find what I value and started focusing on my well-being. I learned and started practising mindfulness, trained as a coach and started helping other leaders in scale-ups facing similar challenges. This book continues my efforts to help others thrive and avoid the pain I and several others faced and continue to face.

When you look for guidance on scale-ups, you will find books and content that talk about how to scale a business, how to build a great culture or how best to protect your mental health as a founder. However, there is hardly any advice on how new-to-scale-up leaders, employees and founders can thrive in this complex environment. Yet, the most successful scale-up leaders will tell you that their emotional skills have been the key reason for their success, and the opposite is also sadly true. Without these skills, intelligent people will fail in scale-ups, break down and question themselves. I've been there and done that. Even with a Cambridge MBA and years at Amazon, I found myself quietly questioning my worth—blaming myself when none was needed It is painful at its best and mental health damaging at its worst. I know several of my ex-colleagues, friends and coachees have gone through this cycle of self-blame, job hopping and – in some cases – deciding not to work in scale-ups anymore. There is nothing wrong with these decisions, but with the right awareness, tools and guidance, you will be more confident, happier and successful in whatever you choose. The most common response to early versions of my book from experienced scale-up leaders (current and former) has been, "I wish I had read this xx years ago before I joined scale-ups."

Through this book, I want to help anyone transitioning to scale-ups, and their managers, coaches and leaders, understand the inherent challenges and find ways to overcome them, so they can truly thrive.

Note

1 All names are modified for anonymity.

Chapter 2

Who this book is for

This book is for

- People looking to transition to scale-ups after having worked in bigger businesses. Perhaps, after several years in big tech, you are now to looking to transition to a more senior role in a scale-up.
- You have recently transitioned to a scale-up from a bigger one and are struggling to navigate the complex environment.
- A relatively green job seeker (Grad/Post-Grad/MBA) deciding where to start your career and has been thinking about joining scale-ups.
- You are an HR leader or a coach supporting scale-up leaders and employees.
- A scale-up leader or a founder who wants to build a better culture within your business.

If you've recently joined or are about to enter a scale-up after a career in the corporate world, buckle up because it will be a wild ride. Prepare for everything you thought you knew about working to be challenged. Scale-ups attract great people who are ambitious, driven, hard-working and looking for excitement, ownership, freedom and greater reward. Yes, you can have it all, but it often comes at a price – confusion, politics, inconsistency, uncertainty. That's why many of us who join scale-ups burn out, quit, or fail to stay the course. But it doesn't have to be like that. You can succeed in this new and unfamiliar environment with your eyes open and the right tools and approach.

Yes, you can have it all, but it often comes at a price – confusion, politics, inconsistency, uncertainty. That's why many of us who join scale-ups burnout, quit, or fail to stay the course.

DOI: 10.4324/9781003565598-3

If you are in the interview stage, well done getting this book at precisely the right time. You certainly have an edge over others. This book will help you from the time you apply to your first year of settling in the business. Using the real-life examples and tips in this book, you will be best positioned to prepare for the interview and assess your future employer, understand the team dynamics and patterns in your first 90 days, and build your support system to succeed in your first year and beyond.

If you are in your early days, perhaps you are struggling to handle a challenging boss, the founder's loyalty to the founding team, the lack of big thinking, or a clash for power. These challenges might be keeping you awake at night and stopping you from making the impact you were hired for in the first place. If this resonates with you, this book is for you.

If you are early in your career or a first-time job seeker, this book will help you assess your suitability to work in the exciting world of scale-ups and help prepare you for the hiring stage and beyond, to truly set you up for success in your career.

Suppose you are a founder, a senior leader, or an HR leader working in scale-ups for a few years; this book will help you support your team in managing team dynamics challenges to deliver their best work, without being constrained by them. You will soon be able to quickly identify patterns and using the tools and strategies in this book, you can move towards solutions faster. You will be able to create a truly winning culture where your employees are growing and thriving.

In this book, I have gathered insights and wisdom from various sources: My own experience, real stories of success and failures from a dozen scale-up leaders, insights and frameworks from thought leaders and findings from various data sources. As a coach, I know how invaluable these stories and insights are. Think of these case studies like a rare opportunity to be mentored by my interviewees, who are all highly respected industry leaders and veterans. Here, you have their untold stories, lessons and tools in your hand. This book doesn't stop with sharing insights; it gives you the practical tools to apply in real life so you can progress confidently no matter what scale-ups throw at you.

Think of this book as a set of equipment you will carry for challenging mountain climbing. The equipment will not teach you to climb but will support you in overcoming challenges during your climb, so you reach your destination skilfully and safely. Reach your summit with a smile, and then aim higher next time.

Chapter 3

How to read this book

The book is structured as follows:

- Part I: Introduction
- Part II: Scale-ups: Understand the space
- Part III: Learn to navigate scale-ups like a pro
- Part IV: Learn from real-life stories
- Part V: Let's focus on YOU
- Part VI: Conclusion: How to turn insights into practice

I recommend that everyone reads the introduction and conclusion, and I hope most readers find the time to read all of this relatively short book. However, if you are time-constrained, here are some tips.

If you are thinking about joining a scale-up, interviewing for one, or have just joined one, **Parts II, III, and IV** will help you make your decision, transition and set yourself up for success. You will be well-equipped with knowledge and tools for those impactful interviews or early days, and this book will give you an edge over someone who hasn't read it. You will thank me later, so you're welcome in advance 🙂.

If you have a few too many years of scale-up experience but are not quite sure if you are in the right place or proper role or working with the right people, **Parts IV and V** will help you gain clarity. I am sure the stories of struggles will resonate with you, and you will learn from the stories of thriving. You will gain clarity on how to transform from within and decide your next steps with confidence.

If you use this book as a reference, reread the conclusion chapter and work through the exercises. The learnings and tools become more relevant as you navigate different challenges and opportunities.

For skim readers (I get it!), you can follow the **highlighted text** to decide which parts to read fully.

I hope this book is enjoyable for you and helps you thrive.

DOI: 10.4324/9781003565598-4

Part II

Scale-ups

Understand the space

Chapter 4

What scale-ups are

Before diving deep into the world of scale-ups, let's clarify what we are discussing.

The term "scale-up" is not widely understood outside the world of scale-ups. For this reason, I debated whether to use this term in my book title, but I decided to go with it because I felt that the people who would get the most value from this book would undoubtedly be familiar with it.

> Scale-ups are like the teenage stage of a high-potential business. When the growth spurt happens, everything gets chaotic, leading to a transformation into adulthood.

But unlike human development, there is no guarantee that a business will develop from a baby to a toddler, then to a child, teenager and fully grown adult. Many businesses die in their early stages, some get stuck or choose to remain in certain stages, and only a few go through their entire development journey.

According to a report by Deloitte and THNK, the chances of a startup to become a scaleup is around 0.5%, which means that only 1 out of 200 surviving startups make it to the coveted title of a scaleup.[1]

The survival of the fittest continues with better chances after the coveted scale-up title is earned. Research shows that among the start-ups that have successfully built a product and completed at least series B funding, 51% of the scale-ups just don't scale or die-off[2]

There are various definitions of a scale-up.

The OECD definition of a scale-up is:

> All enterprises up to 5 years old with average annualised growth greater than 20% per annum, over a three-year period should be considered Gazelles (scale-ups).[3]

DOI: 10.4324/9781003565598-6

Some define scale-ups as businesses that have grown significantly, are truly ready to accelerate and possibly have raised good level of stage A investment or similar.[4]

Another widely used definition is based on revenue i.e. reaching £10M revenue by the 5th year.[5]

Some define it in terms of team size.[6]

Some compare the evolution of a business to that of a family, a tribe, and then to a village and a nation.[7] Scale-ups can be seen in this context as the stage from a family to a tribe and expanding to a village.

Let's define a scale-up in simple terms for this book.

In my definition, a scale-up business satisfies the following:

1 The product market fit is proven
2 The ability to make a profit is understood
3 The business is at an inflection point to grow rapidly
4 There is a need for rapid hiring and change
5 The business invests significant capital for growth

Notes

1 Menno van Dijk, J. D. (2015, July). *SCALE-UP: THE EXPERIENCE GAME.* Netherlands: Deloitte and THNK School of Leadership. Retrieved from InnovationManagement: https://innovationmanagement.se/wp-content/uploads/2015/09/Scale-up-the-Experience-Game.pdf

2 The big boost: How incumbents successfully scale their new businesses, August 2020, McKinsey & Company, www.mckinsey.com. Copyright (c) 2024 McKinsey & Company. All rights reserved. Reprinted by permission.

3 Communities, O. A. (2008). Eurostat-OECD Manual on Business Demography Statistics. Paris: OECD Publishing.

4 Reiff, N. (2024, June 01). What Is Series Funding A, B, and C? Retrieved from Investopedia: https://www.investopedia.com/articles/personal-finance/102015/series-b-c-funding-what-it-all-means-and-how-it-works.asp (accessed 12 Jun. 2024).

5 From Startup to Scaleup: Your Path to Success in 2024 | 7startup VC. (2022, May 5). Retrieved from 7 Startup: https://www.7startup.vc/post/startup-to-scaleup-and-perhaps-unicorn-startup/ (accessed 15 Nov. 2023).

6 Jonathan. (n.d.). The Four Stages All Successful Companies Go Through.... Retrieved from Scale Up Growth: https://scaleupgrowth.co/blog/the-four-stages-all-successful-companies-go-through/ (accessed 08 Dec. 2023).

7 Townsend, T. (2015, November 2). Reid Hoffman: The First Three Stages of Blitzscaling The LinkedIn Co-Founder Tells Students in his Stanford course: Don't strategize. Your Plans Will Change. Retrieved from Inc.: https://www.inc.com/tess-townsend/reid-hoffman-three-stages-of-blitzscaling.html (accessed 14 May 2024).

Chapter 5

Why scale-ups are important

For individuals

We spend most of our waking hours at work. The shape of work has evolved from generation to generation. My grandfathers were self-employed (grandmothers were stay-at-home mums), my parents held the much-coveted government jobs, and my brother and I worked in private businesses. My brother has worked predominantly for the same large corporate employer during his career, while I moved several jobs across various-sized technology businesses. As a human race, we have moved up Maslow's hierarchy of needs[1] with work. While my parents were happy with their 9-to-5 stable government jobs that helped meet ends, today's young people look for more meaning, growth and joy at work while also preserving their lives outside of work. Scale-ups provide opportunities that cannot be found in corporate jobs, such as fast growth, steep learning curve, attractive compensation including share options, flexibility, vibrant culture, workforce, exposure to the latest technology, lack of bureaucracy, etc.

> The thought of doing the same task/job for a lifetime and expecting to earn a predetermined income just enough to meet ends might sound disheartening to many. This is where scale-ups bring hope!

For the growth of the country's economy

Scale-ups are critical for the growth of the nation's economy as they attract investments, provide employment and drive innovation.

I will not discuss this aspect in detail as this is not the focus of this book, but if you are interested, you can read Beauhurst and The Scaleup Institute's 'The Scaleup Index 2022' report.

DOI: 10.4324/9781003565598-7

At the end of the year, according to ONS data, we had 33,955 scaleups in place, contributing £1.2 trillion to the UK economy.[2] Scale-ups attract billions in investment each year. This should give you an idea of the magnitude of impact, we are talking about here.

We know that the US Scale-up sector is much bigger than the UK. According to glass.ai, the US has 5x or more scale-ups than the UK.[3]

It is a fact that, we need scale-ups for a healthy economy, and we need them to succeed.

Notes

1 Further reading: McLeod, S. (2024, January 24). Maslow's Hierarchy of Needs. Retrieved from SimplyPsychology: https://www.simplypsychology.org/maslow.html (accessed 12 Aug. 2023).

2 Beauhurst and The Scaleup Institute's "The Scaleup Index 2022" report, Retrieved from Beauhurst: https://www.beauhurst.com/research/scaleup-index/ (accessed 23 Jun. 2023).

3 New Data on Scaleups: Benchmarking the UK, USA and Germany. (2024, May 23). Retrieved from Glass.AI: https://www.glass.ai/glass-news/new-data-on-scaleups-benchmarking-the-uk-usa-and-germany#:~:text=Adjusted%20figuraes%20for%20population%20show,and%20then%20Germany%20with%20102. (accessed 13 Jun. 2023).

Chapter 6

Are scale-ups the right place for you?

There are several great reasons why one should choose working in scale-ups. But no matter how great the opportunity is, you need to find the job and environment that works with your inherent strengths and motivations.

If you are not clear on your best role/job, the Japanese concept of Ikigai[1] can be quite useful. I, also, recommend Simon Sinek's "Find Your Why"[2] book to gain more self-awareness on what drives you.

In this section, I would like to provide some guidance for you to assess if scale-ups are indeed the right environment for you. This is particularly useful when you are considering transitioning to scale-ups, or you are already in it but not quite sure. It's better late than never to make the right change!

If you like change, speed, innovation, impact and growth, scale-ups are the place to be! Working in scale-ups can be financially lucrative. Packages are attractive, offices are cool, and then there are the stock options which can help one become financially independent sooner than your retirement, and if you are lucky, you could become a millionaire in your 20s or 30, and then spend the rest of your life doing what you love, be it work and/or other pursuits. That's the dream most people who join start-ups or scale-ups with. Generally, people who choose working in scale-ups don't like bureaucracy and hierarchy. They like to break rules or better create their own. Scale-up dynamics need to be seen as a spectrum that depends on factors like stage of the business and maturity of the founding team, so not every scale-up is the same, but there are significant commonalities that we can assume to test your suitability.

Let's look at some of the key personal preferences, styles and motivation that makes one more suitable for scale-ups.

You need changes to keep you motivated

If the idea of doing the same job in the same company and working with the same colleagues for the rest of your working life sounds like a death sentence, then scale-ups could be your thing. It does for me—but only after experimenting with several businesses did I discover which stage best matched my skills and motivation 🙂.

DOI: 10.4324/9781003565598-8

But how much change is too much change for you? In some scale-up environments, the direction of travel can change far too often that it can be wasteful. So, change is not always good or bad. The devil is in the details. In start-ups and scale-ups, many employees leave within three years.[3] This is contrasting to our previous generation when most people had one job for their entire life. This is why you should never expect your parents to understand why you are changing jobs every few years!

In start-ups and scale-ups, many employees leave within three years.

The change in scale-ups is not just driven by people leaving and joining, there could be other factors such as new investments, acquisitions, not being able to raise more capital, new board members influencing strategy, macro-economic factors, competition, etc. While changes in these factors can feel like a slight tremor in large corporations, in a small business, this could feel like a Tsunami.

You move fast

We all have a pace that works best for us. As a society, we have a bias for moving fast, but faster is not always better, because slower could be more considered. The key question for you is, what is your ideal pace of work? I, personally, like to take some time to consider before jumping into action, but I also loathe spending too much time perfecting the proposal when one can test and learn. In early-stage scale-ups, every action can seem to take a quick-and-dirty approach, and as the business grows, more data and process gets embedded ultimately leading to a corporate where there are departments signing off each step even before the first step in execution can take place.

If you are a doer, you like to see things in action fast and learn from it, you will thrive in the earlier stage businesses. While at the other extreme, if you are a deep thinker and/or a meticulous planner and would like every t's and i's to be crossed and dotted, you might be a better fit for a corporate job. If you feel you are somewhere between the two, scale-ups can be a good place for you.

Perfectionism has no place in scale-ups. 'Perfect is the enemy of done' can't be any truer anywhere than in scale-ups.

Speed could also mean you will have to get your hands dirty. I remember being asked to post invitation letters to clients on my first week of joining a scale-up as a director. One of my reports who was from the previous generation was appalled by this request from my manager. I didn't think of it as something beneath me but rather than getting my hands dirty so went ahead with it. One of the interview questions to C-level candidates in a scale-up used to be "What would you do if you find litter on the office floor," and the right answer is "I'll pick it and throw it in the bin". There were quite a few who said things like "I'll complain to the workplace team", "I will not do anything as I have other important tasks to do," etc. If you are resonating with the latter, then there is nothing wrong with you, you are just not cut out for working in early-stage businesses.

You are more of a "doer" than a "thinker"

In the Hindu sacred book, Bhagavad Gita, Lord Krishna, who is the God, becomes a chariot for warrior Arjuna during the war Kurukshetra, a war between the cousins. Arjuna is stuck in a moral dilemma and asks several challenging questions to overcome his distress. Lord Krishna becomes his friend, philosopher and guide. One such question Arjuna asks Lord Krishna relates to "thinkers" and "doers." Arjuna, in his height of desperation and distress, asks if he should give up his responsibilities and become a spiritual monk-like person. For which, Krishna replies that we all have a role and that, some of us are thinkers and some are doers. The world needs both. Of course, thinkers have some skills of the doers and vice versa, but you can tell what your dominant preference is.

If you are not sure where you fall, read on.

- What gives you energy: If you love reflection, analysis and planning vs executing tasks and driving tangible results, you are more of a thinker than a doer, and vice versa. When presented with a problem, do you take a pause to understand it deeply, gather information and develop a thoughtful solution, or do you tend to jump into action? While there are no clear boundaries here, you can work out where you lie in the spectrum by what you enjoy the most.

> If you love reflection, analysis and planning vs executing tasks and driving tangible results, you are more of a thinker than a doer, and vice versa.

- Short-term vs longer term: If you are always thinking a few years ahead rather than fixing the problem of today, then you are more of a thinker than a doer. On the other hand, if you are so occupied with putting down fires of today that you don't have any energy or time to think about tomorrow, let alone the next few years, you are an extreme doer. Most of us will fall somewhere between these two extremes.

- Data vs instincts: If you make lists with pros and cons when deciding, hey, welcome to the club of thinkers. On the other hand, if you rely on your gut instincts (which, by the way, can be a sophisticated AI tool), then you are likely to be a doer. The speed of decision-making can also give hints. Doers tend to decide swiftly, while thinkers weigh the pros and cons for a while.
- Tangible vs Abstract: Thinkers often thrive in the world of abstract and possibilities, while this can be meaningless for the doers who are more focussed on a bird in the hand. A meeting of these extremes can be challenging where one pulls towards possibilities and discussion while the other tries to ground everything to reality and action.

Thinkers often thrive in the world of abstract and possibilities while this can be meaningless for the doers who are more focussed on the bird in hand.

- Risk Tolerance: If you are planning to go on a hike, do you research the routes beforehand, check the weather forecast and prepare your shoes on the day before, or do you just go with it? You know where you stand. Doers are comfortable with the unknown and tend to take more risks and figure it out as they go, while thinkers are more cautious and deliberate in their attitude towards risks.
- Communication and Collaboration: Thinkers enjoy a good debate, writing a deep conceptual document or analysing data to generate exciting insights. Doers only care if any of these results in more actions, and they thrive while they execute and generate tangible outcomes, so they talk in terms of results.

We all must think and act most of the time. It is important to understand where your strength is and choose your environment and role accordingly. Scale-ups need both thinkers and doers, but they need way more doers than thinkers. Doers thrive in scale-up commercial and operational roles for example. Thinkers are needed in small numbers in strategy and planning areas. Engineers who write codes are an exception here. The senior roles generally require more thinking than doing, but also requires "getting things done through others" skills. They have the attributes of a thinker, but they code and they are needed in large numbers in tech scale-ups. If you are a thinker but end up taking a middle management operational role, hoping to make it strategic without buy-in from all your C-level folks, you are setting yourself up for failure.[4]

You like to create something out of nothing

Scale-ups provide opportunities for creating new things, often out of nothing. While larger businesses provide opportunities for making things better through optimisation using process and technology. Which of these excites you, could determine where you could get your energy. More often, innovation in scale-ups is driven out of necessity. "Necessity is a mother of invention." Sometimes, the scale-up idea can itself be innovative and that can provide unique opportunities to create.

You have a higher risk appetite

Of course, innovation comes with risks. So, understanding your risk preference is also very useful. How do you feel about facing failures and learning from them – but losing it all and having to start over again? This is the story of most entrepreneurs. Your investment strategy can also indicate your risk appetite – what kind of investments do you pick? How do you choose between risk and return? How open are you to new things? Are you one of those early adopters of disruptive innovation or the middle or late ones?

> Most people tend to say that they like to take risks, but their actions don't align with their words. Hence, where you put your money is likely to be a true indication of your risk appetite.

You like being a big fish in a small pond

Now, one can measure impact in a variety of ways. If you are, for example, measuring the magnitude of impact, then larger corporations will provide these opportunities where small optimisations can lead to huge gains. But if you like making big changes that have a significant impact on the business you operate in, scale-ups could be your thing. Small fish in a big pond vs big fish in a small pond is an analogy that comes to mind. Even if you are a medium-sized fish in a scale-up, you will be tasked with meaningful size changes. This point also leads to experts vs generalists. In larger businesses, experts are more valued as they need people to optimise, and optimisation requires expertise. In smaller businesses, you need more generalists as each member is in a position to cover more breadth and fit into evolving business needs. The better question to ask yourself is "what kind of impact is meaningful/exciting to me and plays to my strength?"

You want to grow fast

The most common reason people state for moving from a big business to a smaller fast growth business is "growth", and that's true. Promotions are more frequent in scale-ups than in large corporations. Salary hikes are meaningful, and more opportunities become available in a shorter time horizon. Getting promoted in a bigger business can be a bureaucratic and political play, and not saying scale-up promotions are fairer and easier, but in general, it is less intense with higher chances. On this point, though, one needs to be careful not to pursue fancy titles, as titles could mean very different things in different businesses, for example, a director in a blue chip business = C-level in a scale-up.

> As a general rule, benchmark your pay when evaluating the seniority of a role, and nothing else.

You want to have a chance to earn big

While scale-up salaries and benefits might not be hugely different from that of corporates, bonus and stock options are significantly more attractive. Scale-up stocks give the hope for unlimited gains, which is something you could never dream of in a large business. If you are moving from a large corporation to a scale-up, you need to factor in the uncertainty involved in working for a scale-up where the possibility of losing your job is very real and saving up for those in-between times. Having said that, working in technology scale-ups can be financially rewarding especially when the stock options/shares increase in value, and you will hopefully find that when you look back that your total package has been exceeding the same level in large corporations for years.

How do you know if scale-ups are right for you

If you are still not sure if scale-ups are the right environment for you, you can try out the personal scale-up suitability checklist that I have put together.

It is important to note that this doesn't cover all possible employer types, for example, consultancies can provide an environment that is a mix of both scale-ups and corporates. Also, the suitability can change over time, so it will be useful to reflect on how you would have felt five years ago or more, depending on your experience. I know some people's risk appetite increases once they achieve financial independence/stability; for instance, some people prefer execution earlier in their career but their preference changes to thinking later. With that said, this can be your starter to understand where you are likely to be at your best.

Table 6.1 Scale-ups suitability assessment

In each question, pick a statement that describes you the best	*Strongly describes me*	*Somewhat describes me*	*Neutral*	*Somewhat describes me*	*Strongly describes me*	
I believe in failing fast and learning from it.						I believe in a considered approach. Haste makes waste.
I would like to spend more time and energy executing than thinking.						I would like to spend more time thinking than executing.
I enjoy taking risks.						I am risk-averse
I thrive when things change.						I appreciate stability.
I am more of a generalist than a specialist.						I am more of a specialist than a generalist.
When choosing a job, the seniority of my role is more important than the reputation of the business I work for						When choosing a job, the reputation of the business I work for is more important than the seniority of my role.
Getting promoted fast is more important than learning from others in my job.						Learning from others in my job is more important to me than getting promoted fast.

Most of your answers fall in the two left categories: Early-stage scale-ups (< 5 years old, < 500 employees)/start-ups.

Most of your answers fall in neutral: Later-stage scale-ups (> 5 years old, 500–2000 employees).

Most of your answers fall in the two right categories: Bigger businesses (>15 years, >2000 employees).

Notes

1 Myers, C. (2018, February 23). How To Find Your Ikigai And Transform Your Outlook On Life And Business. Retrieved from Forbes: https://www.forbes.com/sites/chrismyers/2018/02/23/how-to-find-your-ikigai-and-transform-your-outlook-on-life-and-business/ (accessed 24 Feb. 2024).

2 Sinek, S., Mead, D., & Docker, P. (2017). *Find Your Why: A Practical Guide for Discovering Purpose for You and Your Team. Penguin Publishing Group.*

3 Ry Sullivan (2018, March 7). Employment Tenure at Startups. Retrieved from Carta. https://carta.com/uk/en/data/employment-tenure-startups/ (accessed 24 Feb 2023).

4 TEST: Are you a Doer or a Thinker? Action-taking vs. Planning. (n.d.). Retrieved from Psychologia: https://psychologia.co/doer-thinker-quiz/ (accessed 19 May 2024).

Chapter 7

What makes scale-ups particularly challenging to work in

Working in scale-ups couldn't be more different to working in traditional businesses where many of our parents might have worked, and some of our peers do, such as working 30 years in a large bank or an established manufacturing business. In those traditional settings, the roles are defined, processes and automation are common, and people have gained significant experience. And then we have large but fast-growing technology businesses which share similarities with scale-ups in terms of change and dynamism, but they have established processes, ways of working and higher level of certainty. This is not to say challenges don't exist in traditional or large fast-growing businesses. In scale-ups, they are different and more prevalent.

In a scale-up business, it's common to see inexperienced leaders in their 20s and 30s, who have spent most of their career building their business, fresh grads working among fresh grads, very little established processes or role definition. Add constant growth and change, and you have the perfect conditions for overwhelm or disproportionate opportunity.

If I were to use an analogy, working in an established business is like learning to swim with a swimming instructor in a temperature-controlled pool with floats, while working in a scale-up is like learning to swim in the sea with some novices who are also learning along with you, while you all surf the waves worrying about potential tsunami while feeling excited at the same time to get to your treasure island. Some of you might want to get a surfboard or bring on an instructor but you might be told that the budget is tight, or the concept is not proven or not needed at this stage. Sometimes (an understatement, many times) it is not clear where all of this is going, which leads you to question if you should head back to the shores. While sometimes, you experience breakthroughs that are so significant that you

DOI: 10.4324/9781003565598-9

want to go further down into the sea. One thing is certain, unlike the still swimming pool, your sea is never boring and never calm. If it gets calm in the sea, you know that's not right!

Change is a constant

Well, we can say that about many businesses and life in general, but the frequency and the extent of change in scale-ups is significantly greater than in other businesses. Think about car racing vs driving on a motorway. Some of these changes are dictated by external factors- investors, market situation, competitors and some by internal factors – inexperienced employees, leaders who can't scale, getting the strategy wrong or learning as the business grows, and not all changes can be explained by a clear rationale! Let's say, it is not common for a new leader to fire and hire their team, or someone with no line management experience to be suddenly promoted to lead a big team.

How do these changes manifest?

- Organisational structure: When I worked in big tech businesses, I experienced changes in organisational structure once in a few years, but in the scale-ups I worked for, changes happened every few months. Some businesses change their organisational structure every six months as a norm. Sometimes, it is easier to change the organisational structure than it is to change something more fundamental like say the core product! What this means is that employees experience changes in team and line management more frequently than they expect, and that requires adjusting and adapting, especially if one is comfortable in their current structure.
- Roles and responsibilities: This can be exciting or deflating, depending on how the change is manifested in one's role. Many employees get expanded remits as the business grows while equally many could see their seniority decline, that is, new levels between them and the CEO, which can be quite demotivating especially if one is attached to the founder and takes pride in working close with them. Obviously, one needs to adapt to the new demands of the business, but it can be hard to do so emotionally especially when the new role is something one is not good at or enjoys or takes pride in. As you will see in Anthony's story in Part IV.

New levels between them and the CEO which can be quite demotivating especially if one is attached to the founder and takes pride in working close with them.

- Ways of working: When a business is small, there is almost no need for processes. Up to 150 people (Dunbar number[12]), a company can be managed with very little processes.

  Malcolm Gladwell discusses the Dunbar number in his 2000 book The Tipping Point[3]. Gladwell describes the company W. L. Gore and Associates, now known for the Gore-Tex brand. By trial and error, the leadership in the company discovered that if more than 150 employees were working together in one building, different social problems could occur. The company started building company buildings with a limit of 150 employees and only 150 parking spaces. When the parking spaces were filled, the company would build another 150-employee building. Sometimes, these buildings would be placed only short distances apart.[4]

  So, as the business scales, new processes and systems need to be introduced to manage at scale. More questions will be asked, and business cases need to be produced. More meetings are needed as more stakeholders are involved. It all gets a bit more formal and complex. Adjusting to this, can be hard or exciting depending on your skills and motivations. Some might jump at the idea of driving efficiency and developing new tools and processes as the solution to move fast while some find it all too overwhelming and a waste of time stating how "old ways are the best" and how the business is getting "slow and corporate." The business might need an operating model that balances scale and speed.
- Internal communication: When a business hires its first internal communication employee, it is a sign of a scaling team that cannot be kept engaged by team lunches and stand-ups. Chinese whispers start to appear when communication is left to chance. This is when the leaders of the business need to start communicating to the team in a coherent way in order to drive engagement and foster a positive culture. Things can go wrong otherwise. Of course, talking to a small group in the kitchen vs addressing a big group in a town hall is very different. In a large group setting, our internal defence systems are on high alert, we become more formal and careful while trying very hard to remain personal and authentic. If you are interested in learning more about authentic leadership, I recommend learning about Bill George's Authentic Leadership model.[5]

When a business hires their first internal communication employee, it is a sign of a scaling team that cannot be kept engaged by team lunches and stand-ups.

- Culture and values: Initially, the culture and values of the business tends to be the same as that of the founder. As the business scales, while the essence remains, it gets bigger than the founder. The group culture and values evolve as the business grows and with conscious efforts to establish, grow and maintain them through new leadership role-modelling and communication. For example, while hustling might be a key value in the early stages, it could change to scaling as the business expands, and now all those hustlers need to find a way to learn to scale or may find themselves a misfit.
- Strategy: The ambition, vision, mission and strategy of scale-ups could evolve too, that is if they had a clear one to start with. This could mean new acquisitions, new markets, closing business units, focus on profitability etc. These changes can bring a whole load of repercussions where some heroes/heroines become zeroes and vice versa. Say, if one is a product manager and finds their product is no longer needed, it can be heartbreaking.
- Investors/Funding: This is probably something most employees will not be exposed to, but nonetheless, can impact their livelihood and job satisfaction. New investors can bring new opportunities and challenges. That is, if the business manages to attract new investors. Struggling to get more funding can be devastating.

The pressure to meet investor expectations can make a scale-up environment toxic while a supportive investor can make the journey so much more worthwhile.

Inexperienced leaders

Not all but many scale-up leaders can be inexperienced, especially in the earlier stages of scale-ups and many scale-ups are led by a first-time founder CEO. This presents its own challenges.

- Lack of clear strategy: While founders are likely to have a strong vision, conviction and bias for action, many of them might not be strategic. This means how they will get to their vision is unclear in the longer term. This could lead to a short-term focussed dynamic that can result in unnecessary flip-turns and changes. Even when they hire strategic employees, they might find them disconnected from reality, theoretical, not detailed enough or not having enough bias for action, and hence decide to fire them, or don't listen to them. The dark side of conviction is that the founders can be opinionated and be closed to feedback. Their

- Culture and values: Initially, the culture and values of the business tends to be the same as that of the founder. As the business scales, while the essence remains, it gets bigger than the founder. The group culture and values evolve as the business grows and with conscious efforts to establish, grow and maintain them through new leadership role-modelling and communication. For example, while hustling might be a key value in the early stages, it could change to scaling as the business expands, and now all those hustlers need to find a way to learn to scale or may find themselves a misfit.
- Strategy: The ambition, vision, mission and strategy of scale-ups could evolve too, that is if they had a clear one to start with. This could mean new acquisitions, new markets, closing business units, focus on profitability etc. These changes can bring a whole load of repercussions where some heroes/heroines become zeroes and vice versa. Say, if one is a product manager and finds their product is no longer needed, it can be heartbreaking.
- Investors/Funding: This is probably something most employees will not be exposed to, but nonetheless, can impact their livelihood and job satisfaction. New investors can bring new opportunities and challenges. That is, if the business manages to attract new investors. Struggling to get more funding can be devastating.

> The pressure to meet investor expectations can make a scale-up environment toxic while a supportive investor can make the journey so much more worthwhile.

Inexperienced leaders

Not all but many scale-up leaders can be inexperienced, especially in the earlier stages of scale-ups and many scale-ups are led by a first-time founder CEO. This presents its own challenges.

- Lack of clear strategy: While founders are likely to have a strong vision, conviction and bias for action, many of them might not be strategic. This means how they will get to their vision is unclear in the longer term. This could lead to a short-term focussed dynamic that can result in unnecessary flip-turns and changes. Even when they hire strategic employees, they might find them disconnected from reality, theoretical, not detailed enough or not having enough bias for action, and hence decide to fire them, or don't listen to them. The dark side of conviction is that the founders can be opinionated and be closed to feedback. Their strong personality might deter honest feedback from their teams, which can breed toxicity and limit business growth.

> The dark side of conviction is that the founders may become opinionated and closed to feedback.

- Inconsistent decision-making: Without a clear strategy and set of principles, consistent decision-making is not possible. This can manifest as pushing in a particular direction and then taking a sudden U-turn, putting the teams who have been working in that direction in a state of uncertainty. Hiring decisions are another key area of challenge where a lack of longer-term thinking can cause havoc.

> Hiring someone senior who cannot scale, means they can become a blocker preventing other employees and teams from progressing. Firing them causes mistrust in the senior leadership, and this cycle can become vicious.

- Limited support and guidance: If you are looking to learn the skills and expertise needed to scale, your founding team might not have it. They are looking at you to run with it or even educate them, so this can be challenging for the less experienced. You will have to look externally for these skills and support, and that needs a certain level of initiative. Many scale-up leaders might not have the skill to manage people, which means you will need to push for clarity on your goals and performance management criteria and seek feedback.

> Inexperienced management can result in unexpected shocks and surprises, e.g., a sudden promotion or being put in performance improvement without so much of a warning.

- High churn and instability: All the above can lead to people churn and instability. It takes time to build knowledge and trust, and a high churn environment breeds mistrust and knowledge leakage, making the lives of those who stay behind much harder. As far as the newcomers, they might find it hard to integrate into an already stretched and stressed team.

Young workforce

Scale-ups are filled with graduates and freshers. The young workforce in scale-ups can present both opportunities and challenges for the organisation. While young employees bring fresh perspectives, energy, and adaptability, there are some common challenges that scale-ups may face when managing a predominantly young workforce:

- Limited experience: Young employees may have limited professional experience, which can impact their ability to navigate complex business situations or make informed decisions. If you don't have enough experienced employees with skills to coach and mentor your inexperienced workforce, you will start seeing issues such as micro-management, reinventing the wheel every time, busy but unproductive work, also known as "spuddle," decisions and actions having unintended consequences, and stress and anxiety due to unrealistic expectations. In addition to this, employees can feel they are not learning/growing enough, so leaving the business or demanding for frequent promotion can be their avenue to experience growth. I remember in one of the businesses I worked for, I was the only experienced person in the whole of the operations team. The whole team was thankful for my presence, eager to learn and felt that I was a "proper" leader – unlike others who had been promoted prematurely, without having truly learnt the skill to coach and develop their teams. Some of the teams were willing to forgo promotions in other areas just to keep put and learn from me. That's how scarce real experience and coaching/mentoring skills can be in some scale-ups.
- Lack of work-life boundaries:

> Young employees, especially those in their early careers, often bring high energy and ambition, but they can also be susceptible to burnout due to poor work-life balance and boundaries.

It is not unusual to find that in scale-ups with predominantly a young workforce that the employees socialise frequently with their work colleagues, date them, go travelling with them etc. Well, that can be enjoyable but when situations change, for example, when one of your friends and colleagues becomes your manager, this presents new challenges in adjusting to a more professional relationship for those involved and/or a feeling of bias/exclusivity for others. Also, workplace relationships gone sour can impact work performance and co-operation. These highly connected networks can become a breeding ground for gossip which can also cause toxicity in the business, which the leaders will have to actively work towards mitigating. Confidentiality can become impossible to maintain. All of which pose additional leadership and cultural challenges.

Confidentiality can become impossible to maintain.

- Retention and Engagement: Most young employees join a startup or a scale-up so they can grow faster, meet interesting people, enjoy the dynamic environment and make millions in their shares. If these expectations are not met, they may become disengaged or seek other opportunities elsewhere.

I once worked in a scale-up where not getting promoted every six months was seen as a failure.

This led to high churn after every promotion cycle, and the management breaking their heads to figure out how to retain the employees and came up with creative job levelling and incentives all of which helped in the shorter term but exacerbated the problem in the longer term.

- Managing generational differences: Scale-ups may have a mix of generations in their workforce, with young employees working alongside more experienced professionals. Managing generational differences can be challenging. In practice, expect divided opinions on everything from what to do for socials to which tool is more user-friendly. This can also lead to synergies and knowledge/wisdom interchange, which is incredible when it happens.

The constant pressure

Working in scale-ups can be pressurising due to various reasons, some of the common ones are detailed below.

- Meeting targets = survival

  Well, there is pressure to meet targets everywhere, but what makes it challenging in scale-ups is that meeting vs not meeting could mean life or death, while in a profitable large corporation, it is unlikely to be the case. Founders are not driven by profit and loss statements. They are driven by ideas and ambition. Once they reach the scale-up stage and have investors on board, they are challenged to drive their business towards sustainable growth, and that requires different ways of operating and thinking to one that got the business to this stage. Missing targets are not taken easily by the investors who are in it for making gains. So, the stakes are high.

It is not uncommon for people to get fired for missing targets even when there are valid reasons for the shortfall.

The business might be dependent on meeting its targets to raise further funding. So, the executives can experience high levels of stress when things don't go to plan, which gets dissipated to the rest of the team too.

- Limited resources

  Scale-ups might not always have deep pockets to invest in automation, tooling and highly skilled people. This means the expectations of employees can become unreal when push comes to shove. During peak sales periods, for example, employees can be pushed to burnouts. And what can be most frustrating is that they might not see the way out of this because of lack of investment in the future.
- The promotion game

  It is not uncommon for some people to get promoted every year in scale-ups, getting fancy titles like VPs or C-level in their early thirties. This must be good right? Yes, but it raises the baseline expectations and status sensitivity of the employees, leaving the ones who don't grow as fast, feeling like a failure. This leads to people leaving or feeling bitter, which then compounds the limited resources issue.
- The need to keep proving your value

Employees are hired for a business need but that need can change/evolve and with it, the employee is put in a position to find their new role and ways of adding value to the business.

Failing, which they become redundant due to no fault of their own. This means there is more pressure to prove oneself each day and reinvent themselves. It could feel like a constant job search, which can feel destabilising and lead to questioning one's worth. Politics can be hard to navigate as everyone tries to secure their role or grow, which could lead to a 'survival of the fittest' situation.

I hope you are convinced that you need special ninja skills to navigate this exciting but complex world of scale-ups. The good news is that these skills can be developed, and the even better news is that the process of developing these skills will result in profound personal growth in all aspects of your life. The question is, are you ready for it?

Notes

1 Dunbar's number is a suggested cognitive limit to the number of people with whom one can maintain stable social relationships—relationships in which an individual knows who each person is and how each person relates to every other person.
Source: Dunbar's number. (n.d.). Retrieved from Wikipedia: https://en.wikipedia.org/wiki/Dunbar%27s_number#cite_note-2

2 Dunbar, R. (1992). Neocortex size as a constraint on group size in primates. *Journal of Human Evolution*, 469–93.

3 Gladwell, M. (2002). The Power of Context (Part two): The Magic Number One Hundred and Fifty. In M. Gladwell, The Tipping Point: How Little Things Can Make a Big Difference (pp. 177–86). Back Bay Books.

4 Source: Dunbar's number. (n.d.). Retrieved from Wikipedia: https://en.wikipedia.org/wiki/Dunbar%27s_number#cite_note-2

5 George, B. (2003). *Authentic Leadership: Rediscovering the Secrets to Creating Lasting Value*. San Francisco: Jossey-Bass.

Part III

Learn to navigate scale-ups like a pro

Chapter 8

How to find and land the right job in the right scale-up

You might be looking for a job in scale-ups for a variety of reasons – perhaps you have just graduated and looking for your first full-time job, you are desperate to get out of your current job, you have lost your job and have been looking for some time in a tough market, you have a job in a larger organisation and looking for more excitement/challenge/satisfaction or you want a pay increase or a higher impact role. Regardless of the reason behind your job search, the considerations below apply. I get it; job search is challenging and can feel like hitting dead ends. Most of us go into it thinking we will be objective, but our emotions can get the better of us, and we experience bias for a positive outcome in the later stages. This is normal, but you need to stay true to your intentions, so you don't just succeed in the interviews, but you succeed in finding the right job. This is from someone who has repeatedly fallen into the same hole! The job search overhead in scale-ups is high – you could spend six months finding a job you are only likely to stay in for two years, if that!

I knew I got there when I started saying 'no' to attractive offers. I hope you do, too.

The red flags

Here are the top red flags that you need to assess objectively.

Validate the business model and source of funding

"You have an amazing user base, but your product is not differentiated. Why would the users pay you?" Cyndi asks during her interview. The CEO/founder of the well-funded scale-up replies with an unconvincing answer. The business was funded well but by investors who have no expertise

DOI: 10.4324/9781003565598-11

in the domain. Cyndi sensed something was not quite right, but the people she met during the interview were all smart and kind, and she was desperate to leave her current job. Her hiring manager has high hopes for the business and her. She deludes herself into putting her concerns aside and takes the offer. A couple of years later, the scale-up failed to raise funds and downsised massively to a limited business model – something she had sensed during her interview.

> If you wouldn't put your money in the scale-up, don't join them as an employee.

Listen to the unspoken

"He holds his team in his hand and pays attention to every detail. His team looks up to him for everything," a senior leader comments about her colleague who is the hiring manager. Her words seem to be positive, but her body language isn't. "Is he a micro-manager?" the candidate asks. The senior leader responds quickly, "No, no! I wouldn't say that." Turns out the hiring manager is indeed a C-level micro-manager. Watch out for cues and unspoken words about your hiring manager. It will save you a lot of pain down the line.

> If something smells fishy, it probably is. Read between the lines.

Pay attention to the culture reflected in the interview process

The interview process is changing as time goes on. New people and processes are constantly added, making it feel like a never-ending process. Finally, the candidate was informed that he had been successful in the interview. In the next few days, the hiring manager contacts people from his LinkedIn contacts without notice for reference checks. He doesn't feel good about this. He joins the business anyway, only to experience a flippant and impulsive leadership approach and frequent judgments and audits behind his back, a complete lack of psychological safety, driving chronic stress. While leaders in bigger corporations contribute to its culture, founders/CEOs are like Godfathers who create and maintain the culture in scale-ups.

> Small actions from leaders are excellent indicators of culture. Be aware.

Meet your 360 team members

Casey doesn't meet their team or peers during the interview, which they find unusual. On their first day, their team is reluctant to meet them, and their colleagues hardly know what they have been hired for and doubt if the role has any opportunity. It was a shocking first day! If you are not exposed to your 360 team members, ask for it! Make sure you get their view on your role. This is crucial to determining if you are set up for success.

> If you don't meet the people you will work with during the interview, you will probably never succeed in working effectively with them.

Speak to former employees

We live in a connected world. In addition to reading reviews from online forums like Glassdoor, reach out to former employees of the scale-up you are interviewing for or, even better, ask your hiring manager to introduce you to some. Your hiring manager's response will give you some clues. When you speak to the former employees, ask them about their experience, why they chose to work and why they left. Listen carefully and reflect on what you have gathered in the process. Do you see any themes? Are there any red flags? Don't ignore them.

> You wouldn't not hire a nanny for your kid without references. Apply the same level of due diligence before joining a scale-up.

Assess your fit to the role and leadership team

She was hired for an operational role, but her strength was strategy. She hoped that would have been teased out in the interview and that she would play a strategic, operational transformation role. Alas, that wasn't the case. The interviewers were impressed by her strategic skills and completely forgot to assess her operational abilities and motivation. While excelling in the strategic planning and scaling part of her role, she was frustrated by the lack of recognition by her not-so-strategic manager and started looking for more strategic roles within the business. Having found none (too early to prove, build a network and move), she left the business disappointed after a year. Don't join a scale-up in the hopes of finding a better fit later or entirely changing the expectations of the role. This can work in big companies with more options to move around. In scale-ups, you need to explore this openly at the interview stage and find out if your role can evolve or if you can move laterally. Versatility is a strength in scale-ups, but make sure you can add value from day one and grow with the business. You will be unlikely to be suitable if you are not convinced this is the case, even if your interviewers decide otherwise. Scale-up founders can be biased towards candidates with impressive brands on their CVs (it's how good their former employer looks to the investors), which can lead to hiring mistakes. Don't become one.

Don't join a scale-up secretly hoping to find a better fit or changing the expectations of the role later – explore these expectations openly during the interview

---

Another flag to look out for is whether the role you are interviewing is an actual role or a short-term project. Sometimes, scale-up leaders hire to fix a specific problem, but they don't think about what happens after the problem is fixed, say in six months. If they are hiring to fix a short-term problem, they should be hiring a contractor. Again, if you have this doubt, ask openly, and the response you get should help you decide with your eyes open. Making assumptions or ignoring your instincts can be costly when interviewing for scale-ups.

Don't try to impress your way in the hiring process; be curious and explore the fit for today and in the future in all honesty.

You likely see one or more of these red flags during your interview. It doesn't mean you should run a mile. You must ask yourself, "Do I feel comfortable tackling this problem, or is this a deal breaker for me?" If you cannot decide objectively, reflecting with a coach or a friend who can provide you with that objective, calm space can be incredibly powerful and then sleep over it.

The green flags

Here are some of the green flags that can reassure you that you are on the right track.

Experienced CEO/Founder and investors

The CEO/Founder has successfully scaled businesses. It is even better if they have experience working in larger organisations before their scale-up career. These experiences will likely build awareness and broader perspectives, often lacking in first-time founder CEOs.

At this point, you might be thinking about the stereotypical college dropout becoming a CEO of a billion-dollar business image. Those are exceptions and if you feel strongly that you have found one, please take the plunge. But we have data to show the below:

> 89% of unicorns[1] had at least one founding member with relevant experience[2]

While this alone is not a guarantee for outstanding leadership, it is a positive sign. Similarly, suppose the business is funded by investors with relevant experience, it is a good sign that the leadership will be supported and challenged by a board that is not just funding them but also fuelling them to grow through their knowledge and contacts. Sometimes known as "smart money."

> History can be a predictor of future success for founders and investors.

The business model and strategy are easy to understand

If you can explain the business model and strategy to your mother quickly, it is a sign of extraordinary clarity. Often, ambiguity is not a sign of complexity but rather a lack of clarity or delusional thinking. It is an excellent sign if your hiring manager can easily articulate how the business makes money and where the growth will come from. Of course, there could be some assumptions and hypotheses in the future strategy, but if they are clear and consistent, it is a green flag.

> If you will put your own money, assuming you are a good investor, in the business, join them.

Consistency, diversity and alignment within the leadership team

When you ask questions like "How can I be successful in my role?" or "Why is my role important?" to the leadership team, and you hear consistent themes, that's a very good sign. It means the leadership team works well and is aligned with your role and the business needs. Diversity of the leadership team is also a great sign, showing that the business doesn't just talk but also walks the walk. Diversity shouldn't exist solely in one dimension, such as gender, but should span multiple dimensions - including age, neurodiversity, ethnic/racial/nationality/educational background (degree/no degree/MBAs), first language and experience (some people with larger organisation experience) - all of which are a great sign. Especially if you are different (read Part V), this one is important to watch out for.

> Diversity in leadership should be something you should see, not just hear about.

The interview process feels balanced

You think the interview is a two-way process, and you are given ample opportunity to understand the business, people and the role, as they do about you. You can reflect on how much you spoke vs. how much your interviewers talked to you as an indication of this. The interview process is neither too short nor too long. It is enough to cover all the bases and meet all your key stakeholders. This is also an excellent sign.

> The interview process should feel more like dating and not like an interrogation.

Rapport and openness with the people you meet

If you can hang out socially with the people you meet in your interview (I'm not suggesting that), it is an excellent sign that there is rapport. When you ask them difficult questions or for former employee contacts, if they respond with confidence, openness and humility, that's another great sign. Even being made comfortable to ask direct and challenging questions is an excellent sign of psychological safety.

> If you get along with the people you meet in your interview, you will likely get along with them when you work as colleagues.

You understand your part in the puzzle

Suppose your understanding of the part you will be playing within the team gets clearer during the interview, and you can already see how your role might evolve, this is another excellent indicator that you are on the right track.

> When it feels like the waves have settled and you can see clearly at the bottom of the lake, you know you have everything to make an informed decision.

Of course, you are not likely to spot all the green flags in any scale-up business (if you do, bingo!), but it's about being aware when you spot them so you can consider them in your decision-making.

Notes

1 "Unicorn" is a start-up business valued at $1billion dollars. Source: Erin Griffith, D. P. (2015, January 22). *The Age of Unicorns*. Retrieved from Fortune: https://fortune.com/2015/01/22/the-age-of-unicorns/ (accessed 29 Mar. 2024).

2 Menno van Dijk, J. D. (2015, July). *SCALE-UP: THE EXPERIENCE GAME*. Netherlands: Deloitte and THNK School of Leadership. Retrieved from InnovationManagement: https://innovationmanagement.se/wp-content/uploads/2015/09/Scale-up-the-Experience-Game.pdf

Chapter 9

What to do in your first 90 days

Congratulations on your new role—this initial phase is often called the probation period. While it is normal to feel pressured to prove yourself, taking a step back and setting your intentions for this critical window will be wiser. I used to feel pressured to prove a lot during my first ninety days in a new job until one of my managers pointed this out quite directly.

"Vidya, no one expects you to prove in the first three months; take your time to understand and learn."

This gave me re-assurance and much-needed feedback not to rush and obsess over proving myself. If you are being pushed to prove and not given time to learn and build relationships, that is a big red flag.

Remember, like the interview process, the probation period is a two-way street, allowing your employer and you to move on if things don't work out without too much overhead.

With that said, what should you do in your first 90 days?

Here are my top tips:

- Understand your colleagues (as humans first and colleagues next)

  Work with your manager to map out your stakeholders and set up an introductory chats with them as part of your onboarding. The aim of these conversations is to get introduced and build trust, so ensure you focus on your relationship more and business a bit less at this point. I usually introduce my journey so far and explain why I joined the company in my role, and I request a similar share from my stakeholders. Most people are happy to listen and share their career journey stories. Once we get to know each other briefly as human beings, I ask them questions such as "How can I make an impact?" and/or "How do you see us working together?" Always give before receiving, so be generous in sharing your knowledge and adding value, even though it might not be part of your job description.

DOI: 10.4324/9781003565598-12

You can also use some tools to get to know your stakeholders better, such as Betty's personal intro template (Part IV: Stories of thriving: The rise of a young COO) or values exercise[1] or journey mapping.[2] These are beneficial exercises to do with your immediate team in an offsite.

Always give before receiving, so be generous in sharing your knowledge and adding value, even though it might not be part of your job description.

- Understand the power in action

  Observe how decisions are made, what role people play in critical decisions, how information moves through the organisation, the relationship dynamics and the unspoken rules. Be curious and observant. Note them down to discuss later with your allies. Not just yet. Map your power stakeholders using the framework in Anthony's story (Part IV: Stories of thriving: From a scale-up leader to a founder) and understand how you can build trust with your power stakeholders and build your power within the business.
- Observe motivations and learn how to influence

  Understand what motivates your key stakeholders. You can observe when they get excited and what frustrates them and/or simply ask them about this. This will help you work out how best to influence them. Similarly, you can share your motivations with your stakeholders to help them work with you better. You can use the insights discovery tool[3] to understand motivations and Baker's model in Part IV: Stories of thriving: The rise of a young COO for learning to influence effectively.
- Define your focus

  Typically, in scale-ups, you will notice several low-hanging opportunities and challenges you can get involved. As suggested by Athena (Part IV: Stories of thriving: How to break stereotypes you don't fit into as a leader), you must put them in boxes (e.g., people, system, process, strategy). Understanding the boxes at a high level will help you avoid being overwhelmed by the details and help bring focus areas for the first six months. Once you define your focus areas, share your thoughts with your manager and peers for feedback to ensure you pick your bets wisely. You can also build trust through this exercise as you demonstrate your "thinking big" skills.
- Identify your potential allies and prioritise them.

  Choose your allies wisely. You cannot make everyone your ally, so be realistic about where you invest your time. You will find that you have a natural rapport with some people and can leverage that to build your trust with them. They are likely to be a bit like you. Perhaps they are logical like you. There will also be other people who will respect you because you bring complementary skills. You can add value to these people and bring them into your circle of trust. Then there will be some people who are experiencing/experienced similar things as you, for example, new joiners/working mums and ex-consultants. This will allow you to build another set of allies. Before you know it, you have your support system. It is essential to nourish these relationships through mutual value and spending time checking in with each other. If you are an introvert, beyond allies, you also need amplifiers. Check Part V for more guidance.

For a fact, you cannot make everyone your ally, so be realistic about where you invest your time.

- Start building your credibility within the business.
  This might sound contrary to my earlier guidance on not trying to prove during probation, but it is not. Even though you are new and learning, you bring unique set of skills to the business, so think about how you can leverage those to add value and help others and build your network and credibility in that process, for example, if you are hired for your strategic skills, why not coach the team to think big. You can also pick your team's pain points and help solve them with your support. You are laying the foundations for your credibility and trust in this period, upon which you can build in the following months and years.

What NOT to do in your first 90 days

Here are some common pitfalls you need to avoid in your first 90 days.

- Getting too focused on delivery at the cost of learning and connecting with people. Your work needs to be balanced with developing connections and knowledge.
- Focusing too much on sharing your own ideas, without listening or observing enough.

Telling explicitly/implicitly that you know better than your new colleagues, way too frequently, for example, "In my past job, we did this."

- Coming up with a plan without getting buy-in from your key stakeholders including your team. It is always best if you can get your stakeholders to co-own the plan with you.
- Buying into other people's opinions/storylines or making assumptions. Not keeping your mind open.
- Taking sides too soon, trusting people pre-maturely and confiding in them orgossiping about others. You need to let time tell you whom to trust.

Notes

1 How to Use the Value Cards Exercise to Help Your Teams Collaborate Better. (n.d.). Retrieved from Viktorcessan: https://www.viktorcessan.com/use-the-value-cards-exercise-to-help-your-teams-collaborate-better/ (accessed 13 Sep. 2023).

2 Schreuder, J. (2017, June 19). My Journey Line. Retrieved from Iterations of Jason: https://www.iterationsofjason.com/2017/06/my-journey-line/ (accessed 14 Sep. 2023).

3 What is Insights Discovery? (n.d.). Retrieved from Insights: https://www.insights.com/products/insights-discovery/ (accessed 18 Sep. 2023).

Chapter 10

How to manage common challenging/toxic patterns that stop you from thriving

At this point, you are most likely to have passed your probation. Well done! Your honeymoon period is over. People talk to you about real issues and stop sugarcoating stuff. You are officially one of them. As a result, you are now more likely to see some challenging, in some cases, toxic patterns. There are several such patterns. I have detailed a few common ones based on my own experience and that of the people I interviewed for this book. The purpose of this chapter is to equip you with awareness of these patterns so you can spot them quickly and manage them skilfully. Of course, not every pattern can be managed or needs to be managed. When something cannot be managed, it is then a case for acceptance or rejection, that is, deciding that's best for you. No matter what, I hope after reading this chapter, you will always be in the driving seat of your well-being and career, which is the main purpose of this book.

How to manage the long-timers protected by the founder's loyalty

You must understand how the founders built their business from almost nothing. In the early days, people around them were the only asset they had. They relied on each other, shared ups and downs as they embarked on the journey of uncertainty with hopes and mutual trust. It is only human and normal that once the business has reached a level of success, the founders still have the loyalty to their early employees and will never trust the newer employees as much as they trust these early ones. So, what is the problem with this? Yes, there is.

Not all, but many early employees' skills that were invaluable in the early stages of the business become irrelevant as the company scales. For example, early startup employees tend to be biased towards action at the expense of finding longer-term solutions that stick. Now, this is a great skill when you are a small team (say < 25) but think about this approach in a

DOI: 10.4324/9781003565598-13

company of 250 employees. Fixing issues every time with an individualistic approach can soon become a major time and motivation killer. At some point, it will be simply not possible to scale without taking a step back and figuring out a scalable solution with the help of solid processes and technology.

Julie is one such early employee who is intertwined in a relationship of dependency and trust with the founder/CEO. The business has grown to 300 people and is looking to expand globally. Julie has also risen through the chain as the business grew and is now the CTO. Julie's strength is her strong bias for action, and she cares deeply about fixing problems and finding solutions quickly. When I say "quickly", I mean instantly! Now, here is the problem. Julie doesn't value longer-term thinking and in fact, she doesn't see it. Julie micromanages her team, is always on and is involved in every decision.

Soon, this approach is becoming an issue, even for Julie. The board is becoming more and more aware of the lack of a technology strategy to scale the business for the new opportunities on the horizon. Julie blames the lack of strategy on her limited bandwidth and hires a director to report to her to manage her team. She hires a highly strategic Engineering Director in Mark. Mark has worked in bigger companies in strategic roles. While Mark introduces strategic approaches, he struggles to cope with the fire-fighting approach and micromanagement from Julie. Julie seems to be happy in the early days with Mark but eventually feels he is not suited for this job. She puts him on a performance improvement plan hoping Mark will leave the business, and when he does, replaces him with Peter who she believes is more aligned with her.

All seem to work for a few months, but soon, technical scalability becomes a blocker for growth. Time and money are wasted. The CEO/founder holds on to his loyal employees at the cost of his business growth. More capable leaders come and go like a revolving door. The pattern repeats! At one point, the board decides to bring new management in and replace the CEO/founder.

This is an example of toxic loyalty where the CEO/founder is not able to let go of his early employee and lets down other people, his business and eventually himself. There is something behind this loyalty that makes it so dangerously powerful. It's scary! The fear that they cannot trust anyone else as much as they trust their "old team."

What can you do

Trying to confront unhealthy loyalty with the people in power can be like stepping on a landmine. Primarily since it is not rational and there is way too much ego and emotions involved. Instead, a wiser approach will be to build your own power to counter its impact on you. You can find how, in Part IV, when you read Anthony's story.

Trying to confront unhealthy loyalty with the people in power can be like stepping on a landmine.

How to manage your C-level micromanager

Micromanagement is defined by the Cambridge Dictionary as to control every part of a situation, project, etc., even including the small details, in a way that may not be necessary and may not give enough responsibility to other employees.[1]

You know, when you are micromanaged, if you generally feel like your manager or leader is looking over your shoulders constantly, and to keep them under control, you tend to over-communicate.

It is the most disempowering feeling as they step in on your toes all too often, which sometimes makes you question why on earth they hired you in the first place. You might feel you have zero decision-making freedom and even on the rare occasions you do, you feel scared about the consequences and grilling that might follow if something goes wrong. Working for a micromanager can be a serious threat to your mental and physical health.

Unfortunately, Scale-ups can be a breeding ground for micromanagers at all levels, but the most harmful ones are the micromanagers at the top, that is, the C-level micromanagers. Typically, in bigger companies, when they get to a certain seniority, the leaders are forced to delegate effectively and stop micromanaging but that's not the case in many scale-ups where "getting their hands dirty" and "obsessing over details" can be seen as a much-needed trait, and it is true to a certain degree given the fact that the teams are generally less experienced and might need some level of monitoring. However, when this behaviour becomes more extreme, it becomes counter-productive and morale-damaging, and can lead to serious impacts on mental health.

Paula is the CMO of an e-commerce scale-up. She has been with his current company for more than a decade and feels very much like a co-founder. Paula is dedicated, hardworking and cares a lot about the future of the business (and holds significant shares) but is a micromanager. To make things worse, Paula is also insecure about her lack of experience in operating at an executive level and worries that the founder CEO and board might lose trust in her. To compensate for this, Paula works long hours and micromanages her team more. Some examples of Paula's micromanagement behaviours are

- Paula gets involved in every decision.
- She checks on her team when they are on holiday by setting up discussions with their reports. While skip-level meetings are a good practice, doing this unannounced may indicate otherwise.
- During peak trading season, the CEO and Paula run calls going over every detail and decision with a large group of people
- Paula monitors her team's activity on the internal messaging system, and assesses them based on their response times, knowledge of every detail and comments
- She gets suspicious when her team doesn't update her on everything they are working on and loves it when they do.
- Paula judges her team every day and changes her opinion on them based on short-term results. Someone is a hero/heroine one day and a zero the next in Paula's world.

The team is also trained to look up to Paula for every decision and this becomes a self-fulfilling prophecy. There is hardly any focus on innovation and scalability while all the energy is used in getting everyday tasks done to perfection. Finally, after serious concerns about marketing slowing down the business and not being set up for scaling, Paula leaves and joins another earlier stage scale-up.

Leaders like Paula are, unfortunately, common in Scale-ups. No amount of meditation apps or benefits can counter the effect of this behaviour on their team's mental health.

What can you do

This is, by far, one of the trickiest issues to manage.

- Increasing your own power is going to put you in a good place to manage your micromanager.
- Beyond that, you can practise non-violent communication[2] to provide feedback and set boundaries.

  Nonviolent Communication is based on the principle of Ahimsa – the natural state of compassion when no violence is present in the heart. ~ Marshall Rosenberg, founder of NVC

Nonviolent Communication (NVC) is a framework developed by Marshall Rosenberg, which involves four steps of communicating:

- What you observe
- Your feeling
- Your needs
- Making a request

For example, when you told me how to execute on project x, I felt sad because my need for ownership was not met. Would it be ok with you if you could provide me an opportunity to come up with my own plan and then provide your inputs. Of course, you wouldn't use the same words, but you get the idea. Communicating in the language of your emotions and needs helps stop the other person from becoming defensive and is likely to lead to a healthier conflict resolution.

- Making some adjustments to create visibility to your manager on key areas, for example, share trackers, progress reports, etc., so you can avoid constant questioning.
- If you have tried everything but you don't see any progress, and if this has started to impact your mental health, don't hesitate to raise it to HR or your sponsor/mentor in a position of power. Also, prepare to leave in parallel.
- If none of this works, hold your head high and walk away. Your mental health is way too precious.

How to break through siloed execution when you want to drive a company-wide initiative

Imagine a leader of a tribe, asks the tribe members to build a castle- a grand one within a year, if they manage to build, they all get a bounty that can guarantee a life of luxury but failing which they all lose their place. He then tasks his leaders to deliver different parts of the castle. The team has never built a castle before and are learning as they do. The leaders have varied skills and experience, some have built different buildings, some have built small parts, while some have maintained existing castles. Now, given the high stakes, everyone gets on to work with their best intentions. Each group builds their parts- one group builds the walls, another group builds the rooms and another builds the pathways etc. They don't talk to each other or even think or plan their work enough because they are too busy and don't see a reason to connect. How do you think the castle is going to turn out, that is if it does get completed? What could be some of the issues?

Bad foundation, incompatible proportions, missing connecting paths, different aesthetics... You get the idea.

In fast-growing scale-ups, siloed execution is a silent killer.

Inexperienced team managed by managers who also have limited experience to execute cross-functionally and/or lack of long-term focus = short-sighted siloed execution.

It's Steve's first month as head of marketing in a fast-growing B2C tech scale-up. He feels exhausted and overwhelmed all the time. Not only is he learning new things, but he is also suffering from information overload. Every meeting he goes into, he observes that people have a list of tasks to do and finish the meeting with more tasks to do. Steve, himself, is finding his task list is growing. Steve has no idea why these tasks are being done, what is the relative importance of them, how they are connected to the bigger picture and each other and the reason for the timelines targeted. Everything seems to be urgent! Steve also notes that the same tasks are being worked on by different people in different departments, and the dependencies and overlaps are not clear.

Steve questions the reason and the priority of the tasks, but receives mixed responses from "yes, we need to make that clear" to "you are new so we understand why this might be too much". He gets a sense, people were "too busy to think about the big picture." The irony is despite all the busyness, velocity is a key issue that is being discussed by the executives. The busyness is not converting to productivity. Lack of alignment to the overall goal and objective and lack of prioritisation and synchronised execution resulting in lower impact at the best or wastage at the worst. Everybody has their head buried in the sand while the elephant in the room goes unnoticed.

What can you do

- Find a senior ally/allies: As a newbie, you are unlikely to have the power and influence to drive the change from siloed execution to more joint-up execution all by yourself. You need to find an ally or even better a few allies. These allies are the ones who will acknowledge the problem and believe that you are the best person to solve this. They have vested interest in the solution and would very much want to be part of the journey. These people could be your peers or your manager or your board. Finding them will make your life so much easier. You can learn how to influence your allies using the tips in Betty's story in Part IV.

- Form a truly cross-functional team: Many programs are dominated by a single function say product, because the sponsor might belong to the function and/or the resources needed for execution primarily sit within the function. However, when there is a need for holistic thinking, you need to ensure that stakeholders from all key functions are part of the core team right from the start. Failing which, you will never truly joint the dots. Multiple perspectives can be harder to navigate but ultimately leads to a much better outcome. Don't take the shortcut by not engaging all the right people from the beginning. This one will come back biting.
- Help the team join the dots: Once you have found your allies and have been empowered to address this issue, you are now going to get your team's buy-in and empower them to be part of the solution. You do this by active listening, asking direct questions with curiosity and providing guidance/ideas from your expertise. You really need to ensure this is not "your solution" but rather jointly owned with your team. That needs time and patience. The patience to watch the answers emerge slowly from your team even though you knew it from the very start. You are coaching, not driving.

Some helpful questions you can ask your team in this process to think holistically and start with the end in mind, all of which will help connect the dots

- What does good look like?
- How does this connect to the company goals and other department goals?
- What is the definition of done?
- What is your expected return on investment for the first year and beyond?
- What KPIs indicate success?
- What are the risks and key dependencies from other teams?
- Who are your key stakeholders?

A simple tool that can help with joining the dots is a single pane of glass (SPOG)[3] which is basically a dashboard or a report that pulls in all key information in one place. For a business project, I use the template on the next page in Figure 10.1 and adjust it as needed.

- Always start with why: You will notice that in scale-ups, there is relentless focus on delivery, which tech teams call as "what we shipped."

Be the person to ask, "why we shipped" and that will change the way your teams and stakeholders think and act.

Project Name: AI-enabled Customer Service Portal

Objective: Improve customer service response time and flexibility for customers while reducing cost of service

How does this contribute to the business goals: Improves customer satisfaction, repeat rate and profitability

Definition of Success

1. Majority of customers use the new portal to seek help
2. Customers rate the new portal positively
3. Customer service cost decreases

Targets

1. 80% of customer contacts are resolved using the new portal – 3 months after launch
2. Customers rate the new portal with NPS > 70 – 6 months after launch
3. Customer service cost decreases by 30% - 9 months after launch

Key Milestones

Q1 2025

- Requirements finalised – In progress
- Build/Buy decision made – At risk of delay

Q2 2025

- Portal Minimal Viable Product Launched – Yet to start
- User test completed – Yet to start

Q3 2025

- Portal launched – Yet to start

RACI (Responsible, Accountable, Consulted, Informed)

R: Ellen R
A: Karina P, Jill K
C: Steve M, Ruth P, Alice N, George P
I: Customer Service Team

Risks and Dependencies

- Budget not approved: Risk
- Customer Support team bandwidth to support roll-out - Dependency

Figure 10.1 A Sample Single Pane of Glass

- Build a culture of joint-up execution: Once you have put the basics in place and got stakeholders on your side, it is then a matter of creating the habit of joint-up execution. You do this by ensuring that every project has a SPOG in place and challenging when you see silos.

How to manage a difficult founder

All founders are certainly hardworking, but many unfortunately are hard work! It takes a lot of passion, conviction, vision, perseverance and risk-taking to become a founder. While all these are great qualities to have and have led to where the business is, they also have their darker sides that can have a detrimental effect on the team and a scaling business. Also, many founders started the business because they don't want to work for anyone else and be bound to corporate constraints. When their business gets to a certain size, they are answerable to the board and their employees and slowly, the rigidity they so loathed starts creeping in. While some founders recognise this and plan their exit, others stick around too long, which causes issues. It is imperative that the founders have the self-awareness to know when to start the business and when they should move out.

Here are some of the common strengths and weaknesses of scale-up founders (Table 10.1). It goes without saying that every founder is unique and hence while this is a useful guide to understand when you see a behaviour, this is not aimed at stereotyping founders.

Table 10.1 Common strengths and weaknesses of scale-up founders

Quality	*When is it valuable?*	*When is it detrimental?*	*Example signs of unhealthy behaviours*
Passion for their business	Helps them work hard and care about every issue.	Too much attachment, expecting the same from their employees, and lack of work/life balance for themselves and others.	Sending emails and/or messaging late in the evening, judging their employees' commitment to work by what they sacrifice in their personal life for work
Conviction	Conviction powers progress by helping them hold on to their idea despite setbacks and criticisms.	Not paying attention to data, experts and feedback can lead to wrong decisions and directions.	Pushing the team to implement something despite several warnings and red flags in data. The team is scared to disagree with the founder on their idea.
Vision	This is what helped the founder start the business, win over investors and key employees.	Vision without operational know-how and awareness can lead to a failed business in the longer term at the worst, and at the best frustrate teams who are left to figure out how to execute impossible ideas.	Presenting a grand vision in the company town hall meeting without addressing/acknowledging major operational issues. What the team works on the ground doesn't have any connection with the founder's vision.
Hustle	Scale-ups need hustle to move fast, keep up with competition and prove to the board. Without hustle, they shall perish.	Unrealistic deadlines, pushing everything to be done now, hasty decisions without considering longer-term implications, too many U-turns leading to waste and team fatigue.	Frequently asking, "Can you do it right now?" Putting down team members who raise concerns about unrealistic deadlines or worst firing them.
Getting hands dirty	The business needed this as a start-up when resources were scarce.	Not delegating effectively can lead to micromanagement of the team and overwhelm the founder.	Wanting to be part of minor and/or repetitive decisions that can be easily delegated. Not having enough time for strategic priorities and/or for their direct reports.

In addition to the above, many founders are inexperienced and have never led bigger teams. This can be limiting their ability to hire the right team, empower them appropriately, communicate effectively to the wider team and bring people along in the journey, all of which are key for driving a scale-up business forward.

Here is a story of one such founder/CEO.

Carl was a lawyer by background. Having worked almost two decades in a law firm, Carl decided to become a start-up founder after he came up with an idea for an online platform. He finds a small team of developers and operational people and develops an online site that attracts millions of visitors in a short space of time. Carl, with his vision and ability to persuade his audience, also managed to attract millions in investment from a foreign venture capitalist who knew little about the industry.

All good so far right. Yes, but here starts the problems. Carl spends the investment in hiring people from big brands in leadership positions, many of whom didn't have experience of scaling. He also struggles with communicating with his ever-growing team. Most of the time, he locks himself in his room and fails to interact with his team frequently. Carl is also not used to being challenged by his subordinates and fires anyone when they do. All of this creates a toxic culture and a business with no path for profitability. This doesn't affect Carl, until the capital runs out. He fails to raise further investment as the delivery suffers and the strategy for monetisation is not clear. This ultimately leads to redundancies, more toxicity and a downward spiral. Carl is fired by the board eventually, but this journey has taken quite a few years and has had a detrimental impact on hundreds of employees during that time.

What can you do

The short answer is it's incredibly tough! However, here are some considerations for you.

- What is the impact of your founder's behaviour on you?

  You might be protected from the direct impact of your founder's behaviour because you might be fortunate to have a great line manager who acts as a shock absorber. While this might feel comfortable and safe, know that your line manager might not stick around for a long time. This buys you some time for sure.

- What is the impact of your founder's behaviour on the business?
  If your founder's behaviour is detrimental to business performance and progress, this is a clear red flag and one that signals you to look at other options.
- Do you have the support of the board (if you are at C-level)?
  It is possible that you are at C-level and have the support of the board. I don't expect this to be the case for most of the readers.
- Is a change in leadership imminent?
  If so, it might be worth hanging around to see if the situation improves.
- How does your founder see you?
  This is important. If you say, your founder's behaviour is not great but tolerable, and doesn't impede progress. Plus, if you hold power and credibility, for example, you are a technical expert in your field and highly regarded by your team and the board, then your founder might behave differently from you. Again, you will still feel the impact of the founder's behaviour on your colleagues, which is not ideal, but scale-ups are not ideal environments, no business is. It's about choosing problems you are ok with, for opportunities you are excited about!

How to stop big egos from stopping you

Big Egos + Big Names = Politics – Action

Imagine you have a ship set out on a mission of finding an unknown treasure. You have some people who believe in this possibility of the treasure and have funded the ship, its crew and fuel just enough to cover another year. Now, imagine that the head of this expedition hires five captains with experience of working in other successful missions where they had played a small part, never as captains.

The thing about this mission is that there is no map and not as much as a direction. There are some potential routes to take, which might/might not lead to the unknown treasure. Every time a captain comes up with an idea of a potential route, another shuts them down. So, the ship is circling around debating which route to take. Six months pass by, and the clock is ticking. Finally, they agree to take a route that is a mix of all their ideas, which takes them only to the neighbouring town. No treasure in sight. The ship is rebranded to become a commuter ferry.

Now, the ship is your scale-up, the owner is your founder and the captains are the senior managers from successful companies. The idea of a ship with five experienced captains sounds great, but it is a recipe for disaster. This is a common problem in scale-ups. As soon as there is enough money raised, some founders set out to find people with big names in their CVs (FAANG[4], Elite universities) in their executive team, but this can become a disaster especially when the path to take is not clear.

- Big titles can mean big egos to contend with
- Big company experience might not be relevant for scale-ups (optimising vs building, structure vs chaos)
- Highly paid execs when put under uncertain situations (and no real work to do) can become territorial, hence breeding politics and slowing down action
- Employees can get frustrated with the politics and inaction, and decide to leave
- It is painful and expensive to perform executives out.

This is what happened to Leah when she joined the e-commerce start-up as a product marketing manager. Frustrated by the lack of clarity on which path to take, her manager and she came up with a proposal and presented it to the Executives. The Executives, who were all tightly holding their positions and quite frankly did not have much to do, spent days reviewing, criticising the proposal so that it became a 100-page thesis report. It takes Leah several coffees and meetings with individuals, and weeks spent on research to finesse this masterpiece of a report. Overall, it takes three months to complete the proposal, three months to get alignment and six months to trial the first few ideas by which time Covid hit, funds ran out and the business had to downsize by 75%, and completely rework the strategy (strangely, the same idea Leah and her manager proposed one year back) with a valuation that was 10% of the initial valuation. If you are wondering, what happened to Leah and the Execs, they all found other positions after wasting a lot of their emotional energy and losing the value in equity.

What can you do

If you find yourself caught up in this tale of big egos, what can you do

- Recognise this is not your problem to solve: This will help you refrain from blaming yourself, which will make things worse for you, and instead focus on managing the situation skilfully.

- Focus on what you can control: It is important to know your limits especially when dealing with people in power. While you can clearly see what the problem is, you might not have the leverage to voice it to the people who have the authority to do something about it. Even if you muster up your courage and confront it, it can easily turn against you. So, it is important to clearly understand your role, who is supporting you on this, who are your "safe" people to protect yourself in this challenging situation.
- Position your work as neutral as possible and drive alignment with the leaders where possible: While you might be working in a function, in this situation, it is important for you to position yourself as neutral as possible. This means listening to all the leaders equally and giving them the same level of attention and respect. Refrain from using the support of your own functional leader as leverage to influence as it might create more friction, unless you understand the politics and believe it will help. Basically, act so you gain respect and credibility as an individual. This is easier said than done but being aware of the broader situation, your behaviour and that of others can help you on this.
- Make your ideas as theirs: This works for gaining stakeholder buy-in in most situations. Give credit generously and acknowledge all contributions.
- Highlight the risk and opportunity cost of delay: Not deciding has a cost. When faced with unreasonable delays, highlight what the cost of it, for example, three engineers are waiting for this decision, which costs £xx per day.
- Ask "what is the worst that could happen if we test this idea": If you are hearing concern after concern for every idea, asking this question can help diffuse the situation and move forward. As a scale-up business, risks need to be taken and as long as the risks are understood, the necessary mitigation actions are in place and the risks can lead to learnings, they are necessary for growth. Ask for what alternative ideas/options people have if they think this is not a good idea. Do so with curiosity and openness so it lands well.
- Time-boxing works! Jeff Bezos categorises decisions[5] as reversible and irreversible to assess how much time and effort needs to be spent on making the decision. This can be a useful framework to use. Don't leave the meeting without deciding or at least aligning on a time frame for making the decision, and then follow through.
- Set yourself a timeframe to review your own options if the situation doesn't change because your time and emotional energy are valuable.

What symptoms will you notice when you have such toxic patterns

- Always on culture: You have hundreds of emails, slack/FB workplace messages and back-to-back meetings in your day. You feel incompetent or FOMO if you haven't read all the messages. You end your day exhausted, only to start doing "real work."
- Us vs Them: There are different groups in the business who feel hostile towards each other. They keep each other out as much as possible, and when they must work together, they don't trust each other and are involved in blaming the other group behind their back.
- Lack of psychological safety: No one accepts their mistakes or does everything to hide them. Even when it is obvious, people don't challenge the mistakes their leaders make. Issues and concerns surface as gossip while everyone says they are quite happy when asked directly. Winning is celebrated, failing is not.
- Busy unproductive work: Everyone is busy with doing "tasks." Tasks that don't align to the overall company goals. Tasks, perhaps, are already worked on elsewhere. Tasks that are likely to be undone by others later. Tasks that can be automated. Tasks that are no longer needed. You get the idea.
- Territorialism: People are more worried about protecting their position than getting the job done, so they spend their energy in batting off people if they suspect them to be tipping on their toes ever so slightly. They are on high alert and at this state their minds are closed for any collaboration or ideas.

All the above, can further lead to the visible issues that are the tip of the iceberg. If these issues are surfacing, it is already too late! If you are a leader reading this, look out for the early patterns so you can fix them before they become symptoms or worse real problems below.

- Employee churn: Scale-up tenures are generally shorter, but it is a red flag if new hires leave within their first year, especially at a senior level, and/or the best performers start to leave.
- Poor mental health: People are off, on extended breaks, or leave abruptly for "personal" reasons can indicate serious toxicity in the work environment leading to mental health issues.

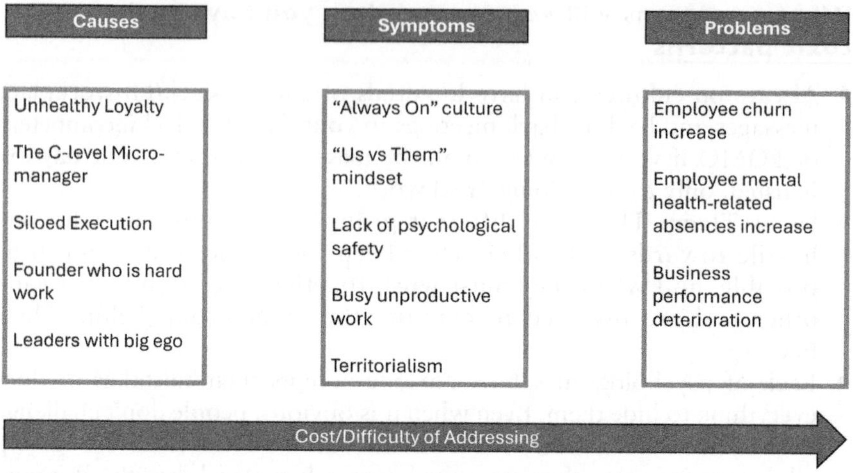

Figure 10.2 Common Toxic Patterns, Symptoms and Problems

Figure 10.2 illustrates this.

Notes

1 micromanage. (n.d.). Retrieved from Cambridge Dictionary: https://dictionary.cambridge.org/dictionary/english/micromanage (accessed 28 Sep. 2023).
2 Rosenberg, M. B. (n.d.). Introduction to NVC. Retrieved from Center for Nonviolent Communication (CNVC): https://www.cnvc.org/learn/what-is-nvc#:~:text=Nonviolent%20Communication%20is%20a%20way,and%20the%20process%20of%20NVC. (accessed 20 Jan. 2024).
3 *What is Single Pane of Glass?* | IBM. (n.d.). Www.ibm.com. https://www.ibm.com/topics/single-pane-of-glass. (accessed 25 Jan. 2024).
4 FAANG: Facebook, Apple, Amazon, Netflix, Google
5 Startup Archive. (2024, January 14). Jeff Bezos Explains One-Way Door Decisions and Two-Way Door Decisions. YouTube. https://www.youtube.com/watch?v=rxsdOQa_QkM

Chapter 11

Special note for founders/ co-founders

If you are a founder or a co-founder reading this book, well done for choosing to invest your time in this topic, amidst your hectic schedules. I know you are juggling, carrying a lot of responsibility on your shoulders and learning as you go towards the path of realising your vision. It's not a path for all and the fact that you have chosen this, says something about you. With those strong admirable qualities come shadows too – ones you need to recognise and address for your own sake, for the sake of your business and, more importantly, for your team and their families. If you really care about the well-being of your employees and prioritise building a healthy culture in your business, read on.

Know your limitations

I am sure you know your strengths. They have gotten you to where you are now, but do you know your limitations? Perhaps, you are not strategic enough or have no experience of working in a bigger organisation or lack the skills to manage a team with compassion. These limitations can profoundly impact the success of the business, your employees' mental health and your organisation's culture. Many founders are blind to it or have chosen not to address it resulting in glaringly obvious issues that everyone except the founder is fully aware of. If this resonates with you, you are drilling holes in your own ship. You need to stop, reflect and find ways to become more self-aware. It is very courageous to ask for help and make decisions that put your business and people ahead of your own ego.

People care enough

Read again, people care enough! As a founder, you want to employ people who care but and this is a big but… It is unreasonable to expect them to care about your business as much as you do. Simply because they don't have the

DOI: 10.4324/9781003565598-14

same stake in it as you do. Your business is your baby. You are stuck with it, and you are probably putting it above most aspects of your life. Your employees, depending on their seniority and compensation, have a role to play but they wouldn't (and shouldn't) put their job above their life.

One of the leaders I interviewed mentioned something she said to her founder CEO, "I am a babysitter for your business. I will change nappies, but I will not take your baby home." What this means is that your team shouldn't be expected to be "always on," responding to your requests out of office hours every day.

Sure, there might be times, your team will need to stretch, but it cannot become the norm. When you send that slack message or email at 10 pm at night or on the weekend, it sends a powerful signal to your team that you expect them to work and care about your business all the time, just like you do, which is not healthy.

Impact matters more than intentions

If you are the founder, it is likely that your team hero/heroine workshops you. They see you as their role model and every word/gesture/action of yours is a powerful signal. I know it is a lot of pressure but unfortunately that kind of power comes with responsibilities. Your actions affect your team's wellbeing. Build a culture of psychological safety so your people will tell you when you take a wrong step and help you course correct before it is too late. If you are reading this and thinking that you have no time to focus on psychological safety while you are under a lot of pressure to deliver, think again.

Amy Edmondson, professor of leadership at Harvard Business School, has conducted depth research into psychological safety and its impact on organisational effectiveness. Amy Edmondson described psychological safety as – *Team psychological safety is defined as a shared belief that the team is safe for interpersonal risk taking.*[1] Her research concluded that psychological safety is a key factor for better team outcomes.[2] This was further supported by a multi-year study in Google, called Project Aristotle, which concluded that psychological safety was by far the most critical factor in explaining why one team succeeded over another.[3]

If you want to build a high-performance team, psychological safety matters.

If you want to assess your team's psychological safety, you can find the questionnaire online.[4]

Build a team of givers

This is especially true if you are hiring leaders from diverse backgrounds. If you truly care, hire diverse leaders who are authentic and have proved that they grow other diverse leaders, not just someone who looks diverse and plays the card to get ahead. Unfortunately, there are quite a few of them around so do suss out the genuine ones. Get help if you don't have that skill. There are excellent DEI consultants who can help.

Adam Grant, in his book "Give and Take"[5] talks about givers and takers, and the impact of being one for individuals and organisations. You want to have more givers in your team. The ones who share learnings, support and empower people – all of which lead to a ripple effect that drives what he calls "productive generosity". And the best way to ensure that is not by hiring a bunch of givers but by weeding out the takers. Unfortunately, scale-up leadership roles can be very attractive for the takers as ambitious as they are. As a founder, you need to sniff the takers out during your hiring process and promotion cycles. Adam Grant suggests that one easy way to identify takers is not to observe them on how they treat you but how they treat people with less or no power. He suggests asking the candidates about whose careers they impacted. He believes the takers will give the names of people who are more influential than them, but the givers will name the people who are less influential than them.[6,7]

The ones who share learnings, support and empower people – all of which lead to a ripple effect that drives what he calls "productive generosity". And the best way to ensure that is not by hiring a bunch of givers but by weeding out the takers.

Let go of unhealthy loyalty and fixed mindset

When faced with a crisis, most people look back at the time when they thrived and try to emulate it to overcome the crisis. For founders, this is likely to be the early stages of their business surrounded by their "good old team." However, a scale-up is so different from a start-up so the start-up gang and approaches are unlikely to help. This is where most founders fail and end up losing their best employees. In the pursuit of bringing back old times, don't lose your current star employees that meet your current business needs and more importantly those who can scale the business up for the future. These are your change drivers so empower them to make the changes, however uncomfortable these changes are for you and your loyal old team members.

Know when to step down

This is a difficult pill to swallow if your job and business are your identity, but many scale-ups have hit the ceiling due to this "Founder CEO conundrum." I am not going to mince my words on this. Simply put, as a founder, you were amazing but as a CEO of a larger organisation, you have run out of your depths, and this is not a problem that can be solved overnight with a coaching programme, a course or by surrounding yourself with smart people (I assume you have tried all these already). This problem has only one solution – your business needs a better leader, and you need to step down. Do so with grace. Now, if you want to run a lifestyle business and be the CEO of your business until you retire, that's your option but do so openly so you don't end up frustrating your people and investors by promising growth that you cannot provide through your leadership. Here I said it. You can walk out with your head held high and know your business is in better hands.

This problem has only one solution – your business needs a better leader, and you need to step down. Do so with grace.

Don't get lured by big brand names on a CV

Hire the smallest possible leadership team based on where the focus needs to be. Don't go after people with big names on their CVs. Hire for skill, experience of truly scaling and fit to scale-up environment. Get help for making hiring decisions. Perhaps someone on your board can be your mentor and help you with these key decisions.

Notes

1 Edmondson, A. (1999). Psychological Safety and Learning Behavior in Work Teams. *Administrative Science Quarterly*, *44*(2), 350–383. https://doi.org/10.2307/2666999
2 Edmondson, A. C. (2018). The fearless organization. John Wiley & Sons, 40–41
3 Tamiru, N. (2023, June 27). Team Dynamics: Five Keys to Building Effective Teams. Think with Google; ThinkwithGoogle. https://www.thinkwithgoogle.com/intl/en-emea/future-of-marketing/management-and-culture/five-dynamics-effective-team/

4 Further reading: Test the Psychological Safety in Your Team. (n.d.). Retrieved from Fearless Organization scan: https://fearlessorganizationscan.com/engage/test-the-psychological-safety-in-your-team (accessed 13 May 2024).
5 Grant, A. (2013). *Give and Take: A Revolutionary Approach to Success.* Weidenfeld & Nicolson.
6 Further reading: Grant, A. (2024, March). In a Job Interview, How Do You Assess Character? Retrieved from Linkedin: https://www.linkedin.com/posts/adammgrant_in-a-job-interview-how-do-you-assess-character-activity-7168031053280980993-JF5W/?utm_source=share&utm_medium=member_android (accessed 19 Apr. 2024).
7 Grant, A. (2016, November). Are You a Giver or a Taker? Retrieved from TED: https://www.ted.com/talks/adam_grant_are_you_a_giver_or_a_taker?subtitle=en (accessed 14 Jul. 2023).

Part IV

Learn from real-life stories

Chapter 12

Stories of struggles

How to navigate when you are older than most of your colleagues and you are not (yet) at C-level

Irina is a marketing professional with 25 years of experience in marketing and product roles across corporates, start-ups and scale-ups. Irina lives with her teenage son. She is bright, well-read and articulate. As an academic high achiever, Irina completed her under and post-graduate degrees from highly reputed UK institutions. She could have pursued traditional career routes in law or management but chose the tech sector – it felt exciting and new. Irina has worked in 17 businesses in both permanent and contracting capacities. The fine line between "exciting" and "unstable" has not escaped her.

Irina describes her experience of working in scale-ups as

> It was absolutely brilliant until it wasn't, the way down was steep and sudden!

Irina transitioned from working in large corporations to a scale-up leadership position as a VP of Marketing. She was ambitious and was aiming to become a Chief Marketing Officer. Just before COVID, she put herself forward for the CMO role but was refused that position. The pandemic hit, and with her industry taking a hit, her career was on hold. During this time, she faced several challenges both in her personal and professional life. As a person with a growth mindset, Irina has re-evaluated her own identity, values and her priorities in her life to establish her career expectations. She realised she needed more balance in her work and life, and chasing the CMO title doesn't quite work with that need.

Irina is no longer frustrated about not being a CMO yet! She consults for scale-up businesses, and her main client is a well-established later-stage scale-up. She works closely with her former colleague and friend, mentors

DOI: 10.4324/9781003565598-16

younger women and has a decent work-life balance. Her income is much lower than what she earned in her VP days, but she is generally more fulfilled and happier.

Learnings from Irina's experience

Don't get attached to status

The rise and sudden fall in your status within a scale-up can be emotionally unsettling. "I didn't see the drama coming," Irina said. Being prepared for change would prevent one from experiencing shocks and burnout from trying too hard not to fail.

Balancing beginner's mindset vs experience

Irina builds on her experience and knowledge but doesn't rely on them entirely to make judgments and decisions. It is important to bring a beginner's mindset in a scale-up environment to every problem and opportunity to truly succeed. Expertise also matters; for example, the experience of working in established banks can be invaluable for new fintech businesses.

The average age of employees working in a scale-up can be in the late twenties. So, if you are, say, in your mid-forties with grown-up children, you have to be intentional in integrating with the rest of the employees.

Find ways to add value

If you are more experienced than most of the team but not at the C-level (out of choice or not), that's not something to resent. You can still bring value through your experience, different perspectives and coaching and mentoring the younger generation, especially on managing work and life. Irina mentors her team on strategy and insights, and coaches younger women with babies on how to balance work and life. This doesn't mean Irina doesn't learn anything. She learns equally from the younger generation on subject areas such as TikTok marketing, online tools to deliver sessions, etc.

> "There is joy in passing on your experience in a constructive and personalised way. Soft leadership is a skill." says Irina with a smile.

Observations and reflections

I see how Irina struggled in her early years post transitioning to scale-ups to balance her work and life, especially as a juggling mother and dealing with blurring boundaries in scale-ups and the drama associated with it. This is exacerbated with the burden on her shoulders to become a CMO in her forties, a target she seemed to have set for herself and judging herself based on it. I can say Irina is not alone in this. Many women in their forties feel this pressure of "now or never" to become a C-level executive. Unfortunately, getting too attached to this goal can start to backfire. Ambition is great, but attachment is not. When life gets tough during covid, Irina realises what really matters to her, like so many of us, and seems to have found her happy place in scale-ups and in her life. What a great example of being a grown-up in a scale-up!

Coaching questions for you

Do you face age-related challenges working in scale-ups? If yes, what are they?

____

____

____

How do you integrate with your colleagues with whom you have a significant age gap?

____

____

____

How can you relate to those colleagues better? Think of some ideas and pick one to try next week

____

____

____

What to do when you feel let down by your leaders

You met Karthik in the introduction. Here is his full story. Karthik is a product leader in his early 30s who lives in the UK with his wife and toddler son. Karthik grew up in a small town in India where his father was a shopkeeper, and his mother was a homemaker. There were not many opportunities for

Karthik growing up, so he maximised every opportunity that came along his way. He manned his family shop since he was very young and completed reading the small collection of English books in the library. Karthik was not a small-town person. He desired to spread his wings to which his family was supportive. He left his town at the age of fifteen and pretty much grasped every opportunity to reach the place where he is now.

Having worked five years in one of the top technology companies, Karthik moved to the UK through an internal job move. He had changed roles internally almost every year within the business. After a year and a half in his new role in the UK, Karthik felt the need to take on a new challenge. He needed an employer who could sponsor his visa for the next two years to get his permanent residentship in the UK. After a few months of searching, Karthik joined a successful scale-up in an operational role in the fin-tech sector. Two months after he joined, his business was valued as a unicorn. His manager and his manager's manager were in their late twenties, while Karthik himself was in his early thirties. Karthik said he experienced "hiring without thinking." People were hired and then had to figure out what they should be doing. Karthik changed his role and became a new market launch manager. He enjoyed the experience of expanding into new territories.

Karthik said he experienced "hiring without thinking." People were hired and then had to figure out what they should be doing.

While his job was going well, COVID hit and like other businesses, Karthik's business started to announce redundancies. With his right to stay in the UK hanging by a thread, Karthik pleaded to his manager that he stay in his job even for much lower pay. At the same time, Karthik started looking for other job opportunities.

When Karthik got another fintech scale-up offer, he quit his job after completing close to two years. Unfortunately, within a year of joining his new job, his manager and his manager's manager both left the business for personal reasons. Karthik was left hanging without support in his role again, and the business itself was not doing so well. So, Karthik decided to quit and follow his manager to a new scale-up in the same space. His new business was family-owned and headquartered in Scotland. With the injection of new capital, they were looking to expand globally. Karthik's manager hired most of the employees in the London office, including Karthik. Unfortunately for Karthik, things didn't go so well for his manager, who had to quit suddenly, leaving not just Karthik but most of the team in London in a state of limbo.

Karthik wanted to rise to the challenge this time. He stepped up to save his London team members as his CEO alluded to a possible promotion. Working closely with the founders, Karthik restructured the team, reassured them and created a new focus. It was a herculean task, which left Karthik exhausted, but he got a sense of satisfaction in doing so. The team also started to respect and enjoy working with him. After about three months, Karthik visited the headquarters in Scotland for a leadership meeting. While Karthik expected to be recognized for all his efforts and promoted, he learned that the founders were hiring Karthik's manager behind his back. Karthik felt let down.

> "I felt stupid for putting in so much effort and caring so much, when clearly I was used!" recalls Karthik.

It was during this time; I met Karthik in a London coffee shop. I have known him for a few years and have coached him for a few months now. Karthik was visibly disturbed. "I am not able to think of anything outside my work", he said. "I have never felt like this. I know I shouldn't feel this way, but I am not able to help it," Karthik continued. We had a chat about what happened, mental health, and his options. Within a few weeks, Karthik had resigned from his job.

It's been almost three months now since Karthik resigned from his last job. Karthik is now freelancing. He is reading and exploring options for starting his own business.

"I can read like sixteen hours a day. Watch product demos out of curiosity," Karthik says with his eyes lit up like a little boy who found his small-town library. Karthik is also looking for new opportunities. This time Karthik wants to focus on the company's mission and ensure he really believes in it.

> "Everything else is noise", Karthik says. "I got offered 2x my previous salary in my last job, but it didn't last. Money is important but only to a certain level", he reflects. Karthik is restless.

He craves change and doing things he can learn from. Where else can he get that, if not from within the ever-evolving scale-up world?

Learnings from Karthik's experience

Reflecting on what he learned from his experience, Karthik says, "I have a problem with authority. I expect too much from them." Karthik realises now that not all C-level people or managers have skills or values he expects of a leader, such as transparency. Having worked in a big business, he expected the same level of management skill, which was rarely seen among scale-up leaders. It has taken time for Karthik to realise this.

Having the right expectations of your management is important to avoid feeling let down or disappointed down the line – this is one of Karthik's key lessons.

Observations and Reflections

Karthik's story is one of a bumpy ride with twists and turns. Driven by ambition and need, Karthik had jumped ship a few times, finally finding somewhere to grow, only to bet let down by his leaders. Karthik is now thinking longterm and being prudent about choosing the right business to work for and setting the right expectations of his scale-up leaders.

Coaching questions for you

Think about a time when you chose the wrong job/business/manager. What was the impact of this decision on you?

____
____
____

What did you learn from this experience?

____
____
____

How will you apply this learning to your future job search?

____
____
____

How to navigate when your logic fails to make an impact

Meet Sandra, an e-commerce leader in her early 40s, who lives with her husband and children in the UK. Sandra is smart, confident and exudes optimism. She holds an MBA from one of the world's top B-schools and has a decade of successful experience in one of the big technology businesses.

Sandra joined the big tech business after her MBA. She grew from strength to strength. Her calm, logical and data-driven approach and her confidence to communicate effectively with senior leaders are exactly what her role required. She got promoted within a couple of years of joining. Things didn't quite turn out the way Sandra had hoped for after her promotion. In order to pursue a career in general management, she was required to take on a supplier-facing role, which Sandra did – but she neither found it enjoyable, nor did it play to her strengths. It was also, during this time Sandra got pregnant with her first kid. After maternity leave, Sandra chose to join a couple of start-up initiatives within the big company. Sandra recollected them as being poorly resourced and copycat ideas that were eventually closed. At this point, Sandra had spent a decade in the business with a very healthy share value and a possibility of a sizable redundancy package. So, Sandra decided to quit and step into the world of scale-ups.

Sandra was looking for a mission-led scale-up that would excite her, having spent the last few years in unfulfilling roles. Her friend, who was working for a sustainability-focused scale-up, recommended a role that she felt would be perfect for Sandra. After interviewing, Sandra was excited about the mission of the business and decided to join them as part of their leadership team. Sandra's role was broad; she was learning rapidly and enjoyed working for a mission-based company. This phase lasted for a year. In the meantime, there was a change in the CEO, as the company had failed to meet the growth targets.

The previous CEO was a visionary and was great at inspiring the team. However, the new CEO was very much an executive who focused on delivering the task at hand. She failed to communicate internally and externally and instead became obsessed with details. Sandra found this change in leadership personally demotivating.

To add to the growing disappointment, Sandra's peers in tech were failing to deliver the automation needed for Sandra's team to execute their plans. Sandra tried to persuade the leadership team including the CEO, that she needed other teams to deliver to succeed, but her concerns seemed to land on deaf ears. Sandra was growing increasingly frustrated. Eventually, it ended in Sandra getting burnt out.

"It didn't feel like there was any willingness or interest in fixing issues. That's what really burned me up," Sandra recalls. Sandra had considered herself as someone with good mental health. It was not until when COVID hit and people started talking about burnout, that Sandra realised that she was experiencing it herself.

"When I was with my kids I was distracted or constantly tired. I was rushing to put them to bed. So, I was being impatient. I had to get back to work because I had something to finish," says Sandra. By this time, Sandra had two young children and a live-in nanny.

"I didn't want to be the mum who was always asking to come in late or leave early," says Sandra.

Sandra then decided to quit. She has since then been advising and consulting for scale-ups in the sustainability space as a fractional leader. Sandra feels she can use her skills to help these scale-ups grow without getting involved in politics or having to constantly influence.

"I think what contributed to the burnout was wanting to do a good job and not being able to do it despite being capable of doing it. It was because I didn't have the resources that I needed, or in some cases, I wasn't good enough at influencing or having the patience for it." *says Sandra.*

Lessons from Sandra's experience

Understanding what type of environment works for you

Sandra grew up in a family where the rules were clear, and fairness was expected. Her dad worked in strategy and used logic and data to influence and make decisions. Her mum was a homemaker and was also calm and even-tempered. Christmas presents were fairly distributed among her two elder siblings and Sandra. Sandra, being the youngest, was also treated with extra care and kindness. Sandra really didn't have to fight for her cause while growing up. Her worldview and expectations were that everyone followed the rules and was expected to be fair. Logic and data were the only tools to resolve any problem. This worked in her first job post-MBA. The environment was very similar to her home environment, but scale-ups were more like the Wild West. Logic and rationale didn't solve everything. People didn't follow the rules all the time. In fact, the rules were not clear. Sandra felt it was unfair.

"If I know that something is right, I don't want to waste time persuading people that it's right. They should just get it and get on with it, and I know now that's not reasonable." *were Sandra's words.*

Now, there is no right and wrong environment. Just find the one that aligns with your values and strengths to truly thrive. For Sandra, working in scale-ups wasn't her environment. She has chosen to work with them instead and that works for her.

"I do not have the patience to bring people on the journey. You're often kind of the grown-up in the room – that's not where I thrive," says Sandra.

Doing your due diligence when interviewing

The scale-up Sandra worked for didn't succeed. Part of the reason was their poor tech and hiring strategies. Sandra felt she went into the job blind. In hindsight, some due diligence on their growth rate, people and hiring approach would have raised some red flags at the interview stage.

It's all about influencing

Yes, it is the "I" word again. Learning to influence different kinds of people effectively is the superpower needed to thrive in scale-ups.

"I was used to logic and data being enough. It's hard for me to accept that when someone isn't following the rules or doing what they're meant to be doing" says Sandra. Sandra is keen to develop this skill as part of her personal growth.

Observations and Reflections

Smart people like Sandra can fail in scale-ups, often not because their skills are not valuable to the business but because they don't have the skill to navigate the emotional challenges and dynamics of this unstructured and unpredictable environment. Sandra loves the dynamism and purpose of the scale-ups she worked for but has decided to stay out of politics. It is great to see Sandra working on influencing different types of stakeholders as part of her personal growth journey.

Coaching questions for you

Does Sandra's experience resonate with you?

____

____

____

Think of a stakeholder whom you have struggled to influence. Why did you find it challenging?

____

____

____

What skills and/or support could have helped to influence this stakeholder better?

How to navigate an abrupt ending scenario

Nolan is a C-level product leader and an advisor in his mid-forties, working within scale-ups. He lives with his wife and children in the UK. Nolan holds an MBA from a reputed global institution and his experience spans from big tech to several fintech scale-ups. He is diligent, honest and knowledgeable.

After graduating in modern languages, Nolan sought to become a content creator. However, that didn't quite come to fruition, and he found himself in the role of a developer in the 90s. Nolan enjoyed the role as that gave him exposure to early e-commerce businesses, however, he found the life of a developer quite isolating. To transition to management consultancy, he pursued an MBA – and it happened. To his surprise, Nolan found working in management consultancy meant trying to look more knowledgeable than he was, most of the time, and always putting his best foot forward. Nolan felt like he was faking and absolutely hated his time there. After a couple of years, Nolan joined one of the big tech companies in a scale-up category and really enjoyed his time. His learning curve was steep.

After three years, Nolan and his family decided to move back to their home location to be closer to their parents, but that meant Nolan had to quit his job and look for a new one. Luckily for Nolan, he got a job as a business manager in a fast-growing FT500 business. The culture of the business was two-fold: There were ambitious MBAs who were pushing for growth while most of the rest of the business clocked in and out. "When I joined, it still had the feel, sort of somewhere between a startup and an old school business", recalls Nolan. Nolan's experience, knowledge and willingness to work longer hours meant he got the opportunity to try his hand at various roles, such as building partnerships and launching new markets.

In one of the partnership meetings, Nolan met the CEO of his next company. Nolan was offered a Chief Product Officer role in a scale-up of 250 employees. Nolan quit his 6000 people business to take on an executive role in a scale-up. Until such time, Nolan had managed a maximum of 3–4 people but now he had a team of 70. It was a real step up. Within a few months of joining, Nolan spotted opportunities and the need for changing the ways of working to enable scale. He formed cross-functional teams by business categories to focus on growth areas, fired and hired people with the right mindset-prioritising smarts and attitude over knowledge and experience-and introduced a data-driven approach to funnel optimisation. His experience in the big tech business taught him how to manage a business using both input and output metrics, which proved invaluable for his new role.

Nolan's collaborative style, open communication and data-led approach were a success in the scale-up, which resulted in the market share increase by 5% in 10-month period without any additional headcount.

While Nolan was enjoying his role and had been in the company for almost three years, a shuffle in the management team happened when the CEO resigned. Nolan interviewed for the CEO role but wasn't successful. He then ended up taking a deputy CEO role with the promise of becoming the COO at some point in the future. At that time, he visited one of their European offices and was underwhelmed by how inefficient it was overall. Nolan, being the open person he was, gave his feedback directly to the head of the business, hoping that it would be received constructively. However, the moment he had this discussion, Nolan realised it didn't quite go to plan and his relationship with the head was never the same. By an unexpected twist of fate, the head of the European business then became the group CEO, leaving Nolan in an unfavourable position politically. Within a few weeks of this appointment, Nolan was asked to interview for the COO role, only to be told he was unsuccessful and that his current role was made redundant.

Nolan was shocked by the turn of events in such a short period. "It was quite traumatic!" Nolan recalls, "I think it kind of shows that in that environment people can wield quite a lot of power."

Despite the abrupt ending, Nolan considers his time in the scale-up a success. After this experience, Nolan joined a start-up and helped shape their product-market fit. Nolan is now freelancing as a fractional product leader and an advisor for scale-ups.

Lessons from Nolan's experience

Culture fit to the environment

This is important for one to thrive: Nolan's values align with an open and collaborative scale-up environment, one where he can speak the truth and be open about his knowledge gaps. Consulting was not one such environment, neither was a scale-up with a leader who was not open to criticism.

Big company experience, especially one from a fast-growth environment

This can be useful in a scale-up context: Nolan applied (selectively) what he learned from his big tech experience, and it was an instant success in the scale-ups he worked on. It helped that Nolan worked in a scale-up category within the big company, where he built new stuff rather than optimising what existed.

Leveraging data and focusing on inputs

Very few successful businesses manage their inputs with the same focus as outputs and use data to do so. So, what are the inputs and outputs of a business? Let's take an e-commerce online fashion business. Metrics such as revenue and orders are outputs, while metrics such as % of items that are available to order, and conversion of their traffic on their site are inputs. Taking care of inputs automatically takes care of the outputs.

Aligning the organisational structure to the focus areas

Nolan, quickly, recognised that progress in new business areas was impossible if the teams had to choose between the mature and new areas, as they would take the easy and safe bet all the time.

> So, he reorganised the teams into mini-business units with cross-functional teams focused on the same goal. This worked like magic, as the alignment led to results.

The importance of being collaborative and communicating with your team

Nolan met all his 70 members, at least once in 6 weeks, by organising 1:1s and skip-level meetings. This really helped Nolan understand what the motivations of his team members were and align them with the organisational goal, which is one of the key attributes of an authentic leader in Bill George's authentic leader model.[1]

Beware of politics

Politics and big egos are prevalent in all environments. The difference between a scale-up and a big company is that individuals in power positions can wield their power disproportionately in the former. In Nolan's example, the approach that worked for him all along resulted in a person in a position of power feeling threatened, which ultimately led to Nolan's exit. I am not sure if this scenario could have been avoided or if it would have been better or worse for Nolan had he continued. However, keeping an eye on politics and power is important to protect oneself and avoid being blindsided. This can be done by collecting feedback and opinions about leaders from people you trust and exchanging information in a safe setting.

One could also take a "test the water" approach by taking a small risk to assess the impact before trying a big one[2]

People can lose their job despite their success and impact

Yes, this is true, especially in a scale-up environment. Hence, it is important not to question oneself at the back of an exit. Not associating one's identity with their job role is crucial to protecting one's mental health and overall life satisfaction.

Susan David Ph.D., Psychologist. Harvard Medical School. TED Speaker. Author of the #1 WSJ bestseller Emotional Agility. Co-Founder of the Institute of Coaching recommends a simple yet powerful approach such as saying "I work as a xx" instead of "I am xx" to avoid clinging to one aspect of our identity, that is, work.[3]

Observations and Reflections

Nolan's story is one of a steep climb to success in scale-ups after transitioning from a big tech business, only to be pushed off the cliff when he least expected. While Nolan's commitment to 'speaking truth to power' is one of his core values and played an important role in his success, the same value applied without fully understanding the situation had cost him his job. I don't believe Nolan would have been happy in that job had he continued but probably could have saved himself the shock and crisis by treading more carefully-something Nolan has learnt from his experience.

Coaching questions for you

Can you think of a time when your superior at work was upset with your actions or words?

___

___

___

How did this impact you?

What did you learn from it? What would you do differently the next time around?

Notes

1 Further reading: Powlus, A. (2017, April 9). Five Characteristics of Authentic Leadership. Retrieved from Pennsylvania State University (PSU): https://sites.psu.edu/leadership/2017/04/09/15415/ (accessed 15 Nov. 2023).

2 Further reading: Deep intimacy, as author Eli J. Finkel explained in *The All-or-Nothing Marriage,* requires some tradeoff between relationship enhancement and self-protection. He asks "are you more willing to let yourself be highly vulnerable in pursuit of deep intimacy, or are you more willing to sacrifice some level of intimacy to avoid being highly vulnerable?" This paradox is also at the heart of the Catch-22 posed by trust researcher Rachel Botsman: Can we take risks without trust? Or is it the act of risk-taking that allows us to develop trust?" Source: Esther Perel, M. A. (n.d.). Want to Build Trust in Your Relationship? Take Risks. Retrieved from Estherperel: https://www.estherperel.com/blog/want-to-build-trust-in-your-relationship-take-risks (accessed 16 Jun. 2024).

3 David, S. (2021, June 3). *Susan David, Ph.D. on LinkedIn: You are more than your job. It's important and healthy to have a strong… | 90 comments.* Linkedin.com. https://www.linkedin.com/posts/susanadavidphd_you-are-more-than-your-job-its-important-activity-6806197853300543488-EXu6/

Chapter 13

Stories of thriving

Imagine you are part of a successful mission. You are surrounded by ambitious people who are all committed to the mission. You give it your all and enjoy doing so. You have the right skills to contribute to the mission and grow with it. You invest much of your time in it, but you know it is worth it. You get growth, satisfaction and an uncapped future fortune if/when the mission is successful. If this sounds exciting to you, then this is how it feels to be part of a successful scale-up and to belong. It is hard work, but the personal and financial growth rate is hugely attractive. Plus, if you enjoy the process of continuous change and growth, the headwinds and choppy seas will not stop you from pursuing the journey.

How to navigate the ups and downs of being a scale-up leader

Anthony is in his early forties and CEO of a well-funded scale-up. He lives with his wife and children in the UK. Before this job, Anthony worked in a unicorn scale-up for about five years. There, he joined as head of sales when the business had fewer than 50 people and left as a Managing Director of a company with 1500 employees.

When Anthony joined the business, little did he expect that he would not only have to prove himself to his boss (CEO) but also to one of his reports, Joe, who was also a founding member.

Joe was a young, twenty-something smart and brash salesperson who had been critical to the business's success. For Joe, respect had to be earned, and authority meant nothing. Four years into his career, Joe was close to his CEO, was already incredibly successful, and had earned millions in equity in one of the most sought-after unicorns.

Anthony recalls how when he turned up in his suit on his first day, Joe did not pay much attention to him (despite Anthony being his new manager). Later, the CEO revealed to Anthony that Joe had questioned him why he had hired "an old man" for this job. Anthony, himself, was in his

DOI: 10.4324/9781003565598-17

early thirties then. Adept at reading the room, Anthony understood Joe's power in the business. He set out to prove himself to Joe for the first three months. He ditched his suit and started proving himself by expanding the company into two key regions. The results started coming in. Joe started to respect Anthony, and they found a way to work together, building on their relative strengths and preferences.

With Joe's support, within a year, Anthony was promoted to the General Manager of the UK and became the right-hand man to the CEO. Press releases, visibility in the company's all-hands meetings and media publicity followed his impressive performance. Anthony was having the time of his life. The thing about scale-ups is that power dynamics constantly shift in line with the evolving needs of the business. A leader is a hero one year, and replaced in that position the next. Enter Richard, who was hired to lead the new markets.

Richard could not have been more different from Anthony. He is calm, controlled and structured in his style. However, unlike Anthony, Richard is not great at reading the room.

Richard's analytical and controlled approach meant he was promoted to COO but failed to win Anthony's trust and support. This becomes a problem as the business is now divided by an "us vs them" mindset. When Richard tries to consolidate all countries, including the UK, under his leadership, Anthony vehemently opposed the move and threatens to leave. Anthony held the key to more than half of the business's revenue. The power struggle ends with Richard leaving the company.

While Anthony was still playing a key delivery role, the CEO is looking for someone like Richard who can work with Anthony to lead the business as COO. This time, the candidate comes from Anthony's area. Anthony hired an exceptionally numerically talented individual named Anand from a large, successful business, with impressive credentials such as an Ivy League degree, on his CV. Within the first year, Anand impresses the CEO and found a way to work with Anthony. While it was hard to accept someone junior and new to take on a more senior position than himself, Anthony conceded and decided to support Anand.

Anand was tactical, lets Anthony keep control of the UK, and giving him due respect while focusing his energy on other low-hanging fruits.

By this time, Anthony was four years into the business, and the company had grown to a scale that required more structure, processes and specialisation – areas that were not Anthony's strong suit. New leaders were hired, and a new executive team was put in place. Anthony no longer held the same fame or power, i.e., he was no longer made to feel special. He knew he needed to leave, but he held on. This made him feel frustrated, and finally, in his fifth year, Anthony left to work on his own start-up – which is now a successful scale-up.

Anthony's childhood experiences

Anthony's mum was a teacher who, Anthony describes, had a "special skill to make one feel special," which formed the foundation of Anthony's confidence. However, it also meant that Anthony's happiness depended on being treated as special. When Anthony was ten years old, he got an opportunity to join the choir of a prestigious Catholic school. This meant early hours, following many rules and etiquette, and sacrificing fun and free time in return for fame and recognition. Anthony describes this experience as "ruthless" for that stage of his life. However, Anthony discovered that he enjoyed the attention and glory that came with it.

As a teenager, Anthony was determined to break the rules and rebel. Through discussing his experiences, Anthony saw connections between these early experiences and his later choices to work in scale-ups rather than larger corporations.

Learnings from Anthony's story

Develop the skill to read the room

It is critical to understand where the power lies in a scale-up and how to influence the key stakeholders. In scale-ups, the "official title" often means less than it does in more established businesses. Interestingly, what can matter more is tenure, closeness to specific leaders and degree of contribution to the earlier milestones of success – even when you're hired explicitly to move on from the business's past successes.

> In scale-ups, the "official title" often means less than it does in more established businesses.

Have passion but beware of fusion

You need to have a high degree of passion for the business to join a scale-up business. However, fusing your identity with the business can lead to disappointment when you get sidelined. The truth is, regardless of how much one puts into the business, the business is going to kick you off when you are no longer needed. It's far more grown-up to recognise and accept it, focus on yourself and the business and flex the balance to make it work for you.

Ensure your skills complement

You must balance common and complementary skills to make the relationship work with your CEO/leader. This is something you can tease out during the interview process.

If you have skills that are 100% identical to, or 0% aligned with, your CEO/leader, it will not work. Ask yourself – and them – what do we have in common, and where can we complement each other.

Plan for your graceful exit

You need to know when to join a scale-up and, more importantly, when to leave. For generalists and leaders who are experts in getting things done, albeit in an unstructured way, the transition point is when the business grows to a scale that requires scalable processes and specialist leaders. That is the time to move on to your next challenge with your head held high.

Tools

Understanding people of power in your business[1]

If you are looking for a model for understanding power, the one proposed by social psychologists John R. P. French and Bertram Raven is a good starting point[2]. The model was created in 1959 and subsequently revised in 1965 to add a sixth source of power-informational power.[3]

I am simplifying the definitions here for ease of understanding in the context of business leadership:

1 **Coercive power:** This is the power your supervisor has over you. You do the job you hate because they monitor you, and you risk being fired if you don't.
2 **Reward power:** This is the power your manager holds over you. You go above and beyond in your job to get a promotion.
3 **Expert power:** This is the power of someone in your business who knows the ins and outs of a system and hence becomes the go-to person for any decisions in that space.

4 **Legitimate power:** Your executives with C-level titles hold this power because of their titles. When they ask you to do something, you prioritise it.
5 **Referent power:** Say a senior leader has won the admiration of several colleagues for being a role model. Even though they might not be in your department, you still ask for their approval for your new big idea. They have referent power over you.
6 **Information power:** Your chief of staff, who is privy to crucial decisions, holds this power over you. You maintain good terms with them and try to get some information that might affect you.

In scale-up businesses, legitimate power comes with being appointed with specific titles.

> However, someone with a more junior title could hold the referent power through affiliation with the CEO and/or in having a history of success in a relatively young business. They can also hold expert power through their knowledge.

In the example of Anthony and Joe, while Anthony held legitimate power during his appointment, Joe had referent and expert powers. Anthony had to gain these powers by proving his value to Joe and building trust with his CEO. In corporations, legitimate power can be significant enough to navigate, but this rarely happens in scale-ups.

Observations and reflections

I can see how Anthony enjoyed being treated as "special" from childhood and loathed not getting that attention. Attention motivated Anthony to build value and power for himself in his scale-up journey while causing frustration when others stole it away from him.

The key learning from Anthony's journey for me, was how power plays a significant role in establishing oneself in scale-ups and how it can be tricky to understand.

> Understanding power dynamics in scale-ups requires awareness, connecting with people on a deeper level and building one's power to gain trust with those in power.

This is something that I am acutely aware of at this stage of my life but was not in my earlier stages. To all those fellow humans who think your skill and logic are enough to succeed, please understand your power and that of others, and apply your skills to build those trusted relationships with who hold it.

Coaching exercises for you

1 Write down all the people who hold significant power in your business and identify what type of power they have in the table below. Try to identify different people for different powers, and you can have more than one person per box. If you feel that some stakeholders have multiple powers, choose the most prominent one.

Table 13.1 Mapping your power stakeholders

	Your Power Stakeholders
Coercive power	
Reward power	
Expert power	
Legitimate power	
Referent power	
Information power	

2 Rate your current level of trust with these powerful stakeholders (1- no trust, 5- high level of trust). Identify 1-3 actions that you can experiment with to build trust.

Table 13.2 Trust level assessment with your power stakeholders

Name of your stakeholder	*How much do they trust you? 1- low, 5-very high*	*How can you build trust?*
For example, John	2	Share a high-quality update on a project John cares about every month

3 What kind of power do you hold? How can you grow your powers (in intensity and breadth)? Hint: think about what your business needs now and in the future.

How to navigate your scale-up career with a long-term mindset

This story is about an individual who experienced phenomenal growth working in scale-ups. I could feel the palpable energy and excitement from someone experiencing this growth.

Betty is 36 and the COO of a scale-up that has grown by more than 200% in the last five years. She lives in the UK with her husband and a cat. Many graduates aspire to Betty's success at a relatively young age when they join a start-up or scale-up. Let's look at what led to her success.

Betty has worked in five scale-ups so far. Her first job after university was at a scale-up, where she joined the graduate scheme. Her role was to expand the business in Scotland, giving her the amazing opportunity to learn about operations. Within a year of Betty joining, her business was bought by another company. After that, Betty joined a smaller business (which grew from 6 to 25 people) in a generalist role covering commercial, operations and marketing. She worked in that role for a couple of years and then moved to Dubai. In Dubai, she joined a new start-up as an Operations Lead. Her business later became a unicorn scale-up. Betty's role was to establish the operations in Dubai, which she successfully did by increasing the number of employees from 1 to 150.

Betty then took a year off to travel, hoping to rejoin her employer in their UK office. However, she was offered a role that was very similar to her role in Dubai – more operational and less strategic than she wanted-. Betty wanted a role that would challenge her and help her learn. So, she declined that offer and joined another lesser -known scale-up as a Business Operations Director. While the business itself didn't scale post-COVID, Betty got promoted to VP and even got offered a C-level position at one point. However, Betty declined, feeling uncertain about the business's prospects and the level of support she would receive from her peers. Instead, she quit and took a role as Director of Business Ops in a scale-up.

> This was a step-down, but she knew she needed to take it as she entered a new domain

Within nine months, Betty was promoted twice and became the COO of the business. When asked about her current role, Betty says, "I am that person who asks everyone to take an hour to plan for the breakdown before embarking on a long road trip." Betty has introduced several new processes and scalable ways of working in her team and is now her CEO's right-hand person.

Betty's childhood experiences

Betty's childhood has shaped and contributed to her success in the scale-up environment. She grew up in a Scottish household with her parents and elder brother. Betty's parents couldn't have been more different. Her dad was an investment banker, the first in her family to complete a degree. Betty describes her dad as strict, traditional, opinionated, strong, impervious to other people's comments, outgoing and hardworking, but lacking compassion. Betty mentions that although her dad had a successful career, he never let his career define him. He had several hobbies and passions. On the other hand, Betty's mum came from a poorer family and had to adjust her career to suit the needs of her family. She couldn't attend university and was busy with various administrative roles. She was creative, organised, and, most of all, a compassionate nurturer. Betty learned early on how to manage big personalities and opinions. She claims with pride that she was the only one in her family with the skills to get her dad to change his mind. She employed various tactics to make it work, such as waiting for the best time, convincing others by putting things in a different perspective, etc.

Sadly, Betty's dad passed away in a sudden heart attack when Betty was only 21. It was a difficult time for Betty, and a flicker of sadness crosses her face as she recalls it. However, reflecting, she describes how this incident made her resilient at a young age. It also gave her the perspective of not taking life and its challenges too seriously. She applies this mindset to tackle challenges at work, including interpersonal issues.

Learnings from Betty's journey

Betty attributes her success to the following approaches and skills.

Build on your strengths

Betty knows her strengths lie in operational transformations. Due to her extroverted personality, she has been asked to take on customer-facing or purely operational roles throughout her career. Still, she politely declined these offers to continue to work on her strengths.

Use early years to get exposure

Betty didn't decide to embark on an operational transformation path until five years into her career. She tried different roles before deciding on this path. This exposure helped Betty make the right choice and gain a broader understanding.

Develop influencing skills

Betty believes stakeholder management and influencing are harder in scale-ups than in the corporates, given the lack of systems and processes. Betty adapts her style to fit individual preferences. She influences through data to some people, takes an emotional angle with others and seeks support from allies for some of her peers.

Make strategic moves

Betty looks for roles that help her grow and learn. She doesn't choose them based on titles or money alone. Betty is persistent and patient and plays the longer-term game in her career.

Tools

Here are some of the tools for developing superpowers like Betty's.

Personal intro

One of the tools Betty uses to build trust, understanding and rapport with her peers and team is her personality intro. She shares this with her team and peers and requests it from them. 'This works like magic and saves a lot of pain! Especially knowing what annoys someone is quite useful!' says Betty.

See below an example:

Table 13.3 Personal introduction template

Name	*Betty*
Role	COO, Company X
Values	Bias for Action, Courage, Resilience, Compassion, Fun
How to build Trust with me?	By delivering at speed, Taking considered risks, persevering on challenging tasks, Caring and supporting others
What breaks my Trust?	Not following up on promises, being disrespectful to other people, too much talk and no action
My best peers did	Worked collaboratively with me, communicated with clarity and brevity, and had fun while working
I get annoyed by	Arguing in text messages/slack. Pick the phone/use Zoom/ in-person to have difficult conversations with me
How would I like to get feedback?	In-person/on a video call 1:1 with specifics on what I could start/stop/continue and why or written for performance reviews.
I enjoy	Travelling, exploring new cuisines, Harry Potter

If you are not too fond of writing about yourself, you can use other useful trust-building tools, such as values and journey-line exercises. If you want to do this yourself with your team or bring in an external coach/ facilitator to conduct these sessions, you can Google to find out more about them. I have facilitated these sessions with the teams I work with and coach and found that the teams left the session with a better understanding of and trust in themselves.

Influencing

As Betty points out, influencing has been the most important skill for her success. I completely resonate with this, having interviewed many successful leaders. If there is one takeaway, I want everyone to take from reading this book, that would be to develop and practise the skill of influencing!

The first step to learning is being aware of where you are. You can understand your natural influencing style and get feedback from your trusted peers and superiors on your strengths and development areas when it comes to influencing.

Baker's model[4] for influencing is a good start if you are looking for a framework. Baker classifies influencing style based on whether it is a

- **Push or a Pull style,** that is, do you actively influence with all your resources or let people come to you by just giving enough away?
- **Rational or emotional,** that is, using data/logic or emotions such as passion/confidence/fear.

Based on these, your natural style could be one of the four: calculation (pull + logical), investigation (push + logical), motivation (push + emotional) or collaboration (pull + emotional).

It is important to understand your natural style, for example, perhaps you use logic to influence and let the facts speak for themselves (calculation), and that of the person you are trying to influence, e.g., they are influenced by big picture vision (motivation) and being communicated with passion. While you can still use your natural style, you could make some adjustments to bridge the gap between, say, your logic to the big picture and remember to talk about what is exciting about this project for others and you.

While you can still use your natural style, you could make some adjustments to bridge the gap

Here is a practical scenario of how this could play out. Say you are a finance director of a scale-up business pitching to drive cost savings in performance marketing to your Chief Marketing Officer. It makes sense to optimise for cost as the business scales marketing. While your CMO sees the value, they don't see it as their top priority. They are motivated by the big-picture vision and growth. Your logic alone is not going to be effective in influencing them. You might need to suggest how the cost savings can be used to invest in further marketing that could lead to the strategic growth needed for their three-year vision and why that's exciting for the business, them and you. Now, you are likely to get attention and support. You get the idea, right. Initially, this might be a bit uncomfortable for you, but like learning to ride a bicycle, you will soon get the hang of it and become more flexible with your influencing style!

Observations and Reflections

Reflecting on Betty's childhood and current strengths, I can see how the skills she developed to manage and influence her dad play a key role in managing her peers and scale-up founders who can be difficult to convince and have opinionated personalities.

For me, Betty's journey and narrative are perfect examples of how someone takes everything life presents in stride and learns from it. A skill that is invaluable to navigating the ups and downs of the scale-up journey.

Betty doesn't complain or dwell on any of her life's challenges. She seems to have developed a habit of converting "poison to medicine[5]," as the Buddhists would say.

I can easily imagine someone narrating the same life experiences as being unfortunate and, as a result, limiting themselves from the great experiences and successes Betty has driven herself to grasp. And there could be valid reasons for such a perception, for example, being highly sensitive increases the chances of being impacted by trauma severely. However, thanks to neuroplasticity, we can all train our brains to develop helpful habits through repetition and consistent practice. I certainly will unleash more of my inner Betty when I face challenges and pay attention to the window of growth they present.

Coaching questions for you

1. What did you learn from Betty's story?

___

___

___

2. What is one action you can take from it to help your journey?

___

___

___

3. How can you support yourself in committing to that action?

___

___

___

How to transition from a large corporate exec to a scale-up CEO

Jeremy is a veteran CEO/NED in the technology space with nearly forty years of experience under his belt. His CV is filled with impressive businesses - large consultancies, FT100 consumer brands, the world's leading tech businesses, and most recently, the one we will focus on, is a successful tech scale-up. Having successfully completed his stint as a CEO of a tech media scale-up for the last five years, Jeremy is now an NED and spends time in the countryside with his family. Jeremy is confident, articulate and has a visible leadership presence.

> Jeremy describes himself as a "people's person" and is evident from his story that he was skilful in "reading the room," connecting with people, and possessed the emotional intelligence and courage to drive hard changes with a humanistic approach.

Jeremy's experience spans multiple functions and areas- consultancy, sales, customer service, revenue management and launching new businesses within large corporations. Having worked in a large tech business for more than eight years, Jeremy transitioned to become CEO for a scale-up that had just completed its series-A fundraising.

Let's re-wind a little at this point. Unlike the high-IQ, low-EQ leaders who shot to the top in the two decades before COVID, Jeremy had strong emotional intelligence. Jeremy was specifically brought in for his people skills as the leaders began to recognise that the lack of which was impacting their ability to succeed in areas where the supplier dynamics demanded better relationship and negotiation skills. Also, apart from the first three years, Jeremy spent the rest of his five years scaling new businesses within the large corporation.

When Jeremy joined the scale-up, the founder/CEO had decided to step down as he didn't enjoy being a CEO. He was a typical entrepreneur – creative and thrived in the start-up phase of the business. With a new investment company on board and a need for change evident, Jeremy began his journey as the CEO. The business itself was doing well in terms of revenue and profitability, albeit it had plateaued in the last year. Jeremy was brought to change the direction of travel and inject new momentum into the business.

Jeremy reflects that his transition was made easy by the fact that everyone realised there was a need for change to grow. Jeremy leveraged this need and alignment to position himself as the leader to drive this change. Backed strongly by the investors and by building a healthy working relationship with the founder, Jeremy started his journey.

Jeremy spent his first year coming up with a three-pillar strategy for growth as well as hiring great people in his team, performing people who didn't add value out of the business, and slowly shifting the culture to welcome change. He took his time to understand and embed, and prioritised and sequenced the changes diplomatically.

"I need to show that I was not a barbarian at the gate, I wasn't going to change everything," Jeremy says.

Long story short, Jeremy exited the business five years down the line, having grown the revenue 6x and the team 5x, when it felt right for him to move on. The business has made multiple acquisitions, been made a B-corp, and is well-positioned for an IPO.

So, what helped Jeremy lead the business to success?

Learnings from Jeremy's experience

Look for alignment among leaders when interviewing

One of the things Jeremy looked for during his interview is the alignment in the leaders' view and understanding of the business. He asked the same set of questions to all of them – "What should, and shouldn't I change?" and the responses seemed pretty aligned. It was clear to Jeremy that there was a need for change and the leadership was behind it. The environment was conducive for Jeremy to drive the change.

Scaling businesses within big companies can be a useful experience in scale-ups

Jeremy recommends getting experience in large businesses and especially in scaling as an intrapreneur. It has certainly worked for him.

> "I think I could only be successful at the scale-up because of the experiences I'd had in the large successful businesses, and the disciplines, especially the disciplines."

Communicate, communicate and communicate

Over-communication is the key to keeping the team together and bringing them along the journey of change. Jeremy followed this and was super transparent to his team about all matters including the financials.

Small things matter when building trust, connection and culture

Jeremy's, particular superpower, although, he plays it down as "normal" things to do, is connecting with people and shifting the culture by small gestures, be it walking around the office or hanging out for team lunches or wearing a semi-formal outfit or replacing hefty leather sofas with modest working desks in his room. All these actions were intentional gestures for building connections and shifting the culture.

> "One of the things I do every day, probably once, sometimes twice a day, I just walk to the office every day. I just go round and say hello to everyone and literally walk."

Find the right people for your business

Jeremy brought on some successful leaders into his business. Many of them had big company experiences, but unlike some leaders who blindly looked for big brands on the CVs, Jeremy looked for something specific beyond the know-how and skills. Talking about one of his successful leaders, Jeremy says, "I wanted them to help be change agents, who'd in some ways moved around and moved into different environments, so had to adapt and change. They had learnt what good looks like, but they had also learnt how to operate in different environments. Those were the kind of flexibility I was looking for."

Jeremy also points out that managing investors was a whole new ball game for him and that effective stakeholder management skills were the key to success in this area. As with any successful scale-up leader, Jeremy wishes he had gone fast on some of the changes but also realises that this was a benefit of hindsight.

Having worked in so many successful businesses, the stint in the scale-up has been Jeremy's most fulfilling role. "Something that feels more tangible than any of the other roles," says Jeremy reflecting on his journey.

Tools

One thing that stood out for me in Jeremy's story is how he managed to build Trust with his team.

Stephen M. R. Covey and Greg Link in their book "Smart Trust"[6] argue the case for building Trust to drive up speed and drive down cost in any organisation. They have also come up with a Smart-Trust Matrix,[7] which can help make smart judgements as a leader. Stephen and Greg recommend that as a leader, building a smart trust approach - with a high propensity to trust by default and a high skill to analyse the situation and make an informed judgement – is a key skill to deliver at speed. That is, you trust by default until your trust is broken, and you ensure you have analysed the situation/person enough with facts to build your trust. You don't trust blindly or be suspicious or stuck in the indecisive state of whether to trust or not. They recommend building smart trust in a five-step process.

Observations and Reflections

Reflecting on Jeremy's journey, I feel he leveraged his self-awareness and extensive experience, and people skills to drive his business to success as a CEO. Particularly, how Jeremy extended his trust to his team and built his trust with his team as a new leader is inspirational and insightful. He did this by both making some bold moves, for example, people changes and through small everyday actions, for example, Walking around the office, which really helped to drive changes and remain connected to the team while doing so.

Coaching questions for you

Reflect on these questions

1. As a leader, how do you build trust with your team every day? List 3–5 behaviours

2. Think of your current role and a recent tough decision you had to make, what level of trust you placed on others vs relying on your own analysis?

3. In hindsight, what did you do well and what could you have done better?

How to know when to quit

Laura is a forty-year-old C-level leader of a scale-up. She lives in the UK with her husband and two children. Since graduating, Laura has had 8 jobs-three of which were in big corporations, one within a scale-up in a big corporation, and the other four in scale-ups. Laura is smart, ambitious and straight-talking.

> "I have a different view of time," says Laura. "I think different scales of businesses give you a different sense of how much you're learning."

Laura graduated when the dot.com bubble burst with a hefty student loan to pay. Despite wanting to join a start-up, Laura joined a big outsourcing organisation as part of their graduate scheme. While this gave Laura the experience of working in the real world and learning about processes, she felt like she was missing something. After three years, when the opportunity came about, Laura joined a start-up as its third employee.

'I loved it. It was a 24/7 thing, but we were building something new,' Laura recalls. After spending 3.5 years, the business scaled successfully and was bought by another company.

'It got to the point where I was totally exhausted,' said Laura. At that point, she resigned and went to work for a big retail corporation.

While the learning in the big company was steep, Laura found the process heavy, slow culture draining.

"It was like six weeks to the next steering committee meeting, and you write an RFI, for tying a shoelace," says Laura.

Laura switched jobs again and joined a scale-up within a massive e-commerce organisation. She was leading the setup of the UK and Ireland markets. The product was great, and she worked in a small team with a lot of autonomy. The company and Laura grew from strength to strength. Laura got promoted and built a strong team. Having spent nearly six years, her longest service yet, Laura decided to move on as the company grew to a size where it was no longer a scale-up.

After this, Laura joined another big company in its new digital innovation team and enjoyed working there. But then COVID hit and Laura had to move on. She joined another scale-up with a promise of being promoted to C-level, but the founder didn't keep his word. Laura found this lack of integrity and other issues in the founding team incredibly frustrating, which led her to move on to her first C-level role in her current scale-up.

Reflecting on what she found the most challenging in all her roles, Laura says,

> "I think the thread through all of those things I found frustrating was the politics of having to convince people, not because they don't see that it's a good idea, but because they see it as a threat to their role or to their remit or to their previous decisions."

Laura is a strategic leader and that's a rare skill in the world of scale-ups. Asked how she manages to bring people along in her strategy, Laura shares her art of storytelling.

> Everybody likes knowing the destination right, regardless of the role that they're in, whether they like packing boxes in a warehouse or writing code, or they're like, you know, the head of marketing that everybody wants to know. Oh, we're travelling to Mars, right?

Laura doesn't see the job changes as failures. She feels if she learns in her job, it's worth her while. Laura loves change and feels scale-up years are more like dog years. She doesn't join a business thinking that she will stay there for five or ten years. She prioritises working in businesses with great people and products so she can learn and grow. Laura is also lucky to have a secure financial fallback in her husband which not many people might have.

Laura sees herself working in a scale-up leadership role for another decade. "It's intense at times," says Laura, but also recognises that it varies hugely by the company and the maturity of its leaders.

Laura's childhood experiences

Laura grew up in a family where the parents worked hard and yet had just enough money to make ends meet. Having lost their youngest child, the parents didn't expect much from their two children beyond them keeping well and happy. Laura and her brother fared very well at school, much to the surprise of their parents, who themselves didn't go to university. Laura was naturally competitive. Driven by her high-performing brother and wanting to have more money to do nice things in the future, Laura has pushed herself to date.

Learnings from Laura's experience

Laura is a great example of a scale-up leader who has the confidence to take risks and not take short tenures as a reflection of personal failure, keeping her focus on learning and progress. Measuring the success of your role in a scale-up by how much you have learned rather than the years you have spent is the key learning I took away from Laura's story.

It's all in one's perspective and mindset. Another learning from Laura's story is knowing when to leave. A lot of people stay in jobs for too long even though they are no longer motivated, or the culture is toxic etc and Laura did a great job of keeping her eyes open and knowing when it was time.

Observations and reflections

This is something I have personally struggled with. Even a casual comment from someone 'Changing job again!' would trigger unpleasant feelings within me. Over the years, I have developed my confidence in this space. These are some of the things that helped me to build confidence:

Finding my "why"

On one of the depressing COVID lockdown days, I attended Simon Sinek's online workshop. This helped me come up with my personal "why" statement and think about my motivation and purpose more broadly beyond my day job.

Upskilling

Qualifying as a professional coach was a big step towards becoming independent. It helped me believe that I can stand on my own legs without being employed, if needed.

Freelancing

Instead of desperately trying to find another job as soon as one ends, I tried freelancing between jobs. I got an assignment from my previous work colleague. It was well-paid, and I thoroughly enjoyed it. I built a new network and more importantly, confidence in finding interim/fractional leadership roles. Again, this helped lighten the burden of finding another job before one end.

Understanding what you bring to your job clearly

It took me quite a few years to understand what my unique skills were and where they would be valued, but I am glad I got there. Not to say, this might not change with time and experience, but it is important to know your superpower at work so you can target the right roles in the right businesses and most importantly, work for the right kind of people who can value your skills.

Engaging in meaningful activities outside work

Being productive is a big value for me. So, I engage in activities that help me live my values. This is where writing, working in my allotment or garden or decluttering my space helps add meaning to my day. Even when I am not employed or between jobs or experience an unproductive period at work, these activities help me feel satisfied and go a long way to keep my mind and body healthy. Many people lose their purpose when they lose their job. Broadening your activities and network can protect you in tough times.

Strangely, a little bit of distance between your work and you can make you perform better. It is like climbing a mountain without a heavy backpack – the fear of losing your job.

Coaching questions for you

1. What did you do today that was worth your while at work?

____

____

____

2. Why was it worth your while? What value did you live by doing it?

____

____

____

3. What can you do outside work that will help you live by that value?

____

____

____

How to break leadership stereotypes that you don't fit into

Athena is in her late thirties and is already into her third Chief Technology Officer (CTO) role in successful scale-ups. Growing up, Athena wanted to become a comic illustrator but ended up learning coding, moving to the UK from Greece with her then-partner (now fiancé), and has stayed here since. Athena is calm, soft-spoken with a Greek accent and hits the nail on various topics as she speaks from her home office cum video games station. She switches between vulnerability and authority quite naturally and exudes quiet confidence and humility, which is refreshing to see.

Women CTOs are, sadly, rare to spot. Women CTOs with a non-native accent are even rarer. Women of colour CTOs with a non-native accent, now we are talking about a needle-in-a-haystack situation.[8]

In 2020, 50% of workers in the labour market as a whole were women; in tech, it was half that, at 26%. As of 2021, only 3% of Chief Technology Officers (CTOs) or Technical Director roles were held by female staff.[9]

Athena has been the only/one of the few females in many rooms in her life. Starting from her university where she was among the six girls in a class of 80. She didn't feel odd and fitted in quite well in that setting. Athena worked very hard at her university while also doing a full-time job. She had no life outside work back then, but she was learning and enjoying the experience. "Coming out of university, I thought, I'm just going to be a coder, and this was going to be my career," recalls Athena.

After University, Athena found a job in the UK and moved in with her partner. Unfortunately, she was soon made redundant in that job, which put her in a state of financial uncertainty. "So, from that moment on, I was really focused on making sure I'm financially secure," reflects Athena. Athena eventually found a job as a contractor working in the basement of a small business. She was bored but had access to the server and started building software. Athena jumped ship to become a website developer for another scale-up. While she enjoyed her role, after two years, she didn't feel like this would be her longer-term path. "I remember, like today, I was in the elevator coming back home. I don't remember what triggered this, but I was thinking, am I going to be doing this five years from now," recalls Athena.

Athena then started to look for jobs as an engineering manager. Her own manager sensed her need and gave her the opportunity to manage a small team. Within six months of becoming a manager, two of her top developers quit, which was not a great start for Athena, but she took it upon herself to focus on becoming a better manager. She attended external training and coaching in this pursuit but ultimately listened to her intuition and started spending more time with her team one-to-one. "I would work with them to try and understand how they work, and what they do and what good looks like for them," recalls Athena.

At one point, Athena felt juggling her responsibilities as a coder and a manager hindered her ability to make an impact. So, she found herself a new job where she could be a full-time manager. It is in that role, she realised that she saw the bigger picture more than any of her peers. Athena developed an approach which she calls "boxing." She managed everything – systems, people, problems, in the form of boxes. If she knows how each box works, she can move things forward without having to know all the details of what's in the box. "I applied this approach of boxes to platforms, businesses, teams and people management as well. Because if you try to care about everything all the time you're going to fail" says Athena.

After a successful few years, Athena got promoted to a director and suddenly her role changed dramatically. She became the only woman on the board. As an introvert, another challenge was around the corner in this role for Athena, "I was invited to a lot of dinners and lunches with people who we pay money for," recalls Athena. She found this all too overwhelming to begin with but with time she started to prioritise her relationships. Being a logical person, Athena would not pursue deeper relationships with those who were not logical since she knew she wouldn't win that game, instead, would aim to maintain a workable relationship with them and focussed on people with whom she got on naturally instead.

"Logic doesn't always work. I'm very logical. If I met with somebody and they weren't responding well to logic, I kind of deprioritize that relationship," says Athena, while adding quickly that she is not recommending this approach to others.

As days progressed, Athena's role got more complicated with M&As and integration. Athena and her team worked hard and long. It was her first taste of burnout. While the team managed to pull it off, this wasn't something Athena was proud of. "This is the time when I made a lot of bad calls when it comes to priority," recalls Athena. After this experience, Athena took a sidestep joining a smaller business in the same space with what she calls more a "hippie culture". Within six months of joining the business, the CTO and his report resigned leaving Athena having to dive straight into the deep end. "For like 3 months, no one in the company knew how to deploy in production," remembers Athena. Athena spotted someone junior to help her with this situation and set that person up for success. Eventually, this person became the head of platform when Athena left the business as the CTO. Her promotion to CTO came as she found a sponsor in her female manager who empowered her to act as the people leader for the technology team. As an introvert, this was a unique growth opportunity for Athena. "I realised that when I create an environment for engagement with people on my own terms, it's much easier for me to kind of manage that," says Athena.

Athena is now an established C-level Tech leader. She attends conferences that involve a lot of public speaking and even arguing on stage. She does these, not just to represent her team, as she did in her early career, but also for building her own brand. For someone who didn't consider herself "a people's person," Athena has surprised herself in this space.

> When asked how she manages people's problems, which many introverts find challenging, Athena responds by saying, "I see people's problems just like every other problem. Maybe it's something in my brain, but like I just see all of these things as puzzles that you need to solve."

Athena doesn't bring emotions such as anger and frustration to conflicts, which seems to free up time and energy to resolve things with a calm and rational approach (It seems to me that she is using her prefrontal cortex rather than her limbic "flight or fight or freeze" response). When asked about how she manages that, Athena reflects, "I'm never like 100% caring, like in the end, it's just a job right? A lot of founders don't have that distance. They say, I founded this. This is my baby. I'm like, okay, I can change the diaper. I'm not going to take it home with me- you take it back with you." This is Athena's secret sauce. As an obsessive gamer and puzzle enthusiast, she brings that problem-solving, playful approach, strategy, tactics and hunger for the next level of challenge into her career.

Learnings from Athena's experience

Leading as a minority

Athena was often the youngest and/or the only female and/or the only non-native English speaker in the leadership team. There were times when the senior engineers would not respect her due to these attributes.

> Athena made sure she established her authority through a variety of approaches including talking about her experience, skills, seniority and confronting the bullies. She preferred to tackle them directly rather than escalating.

Building your own confidence and support system

Athena's success can be attributed to two things, in her own words, "I think two things that made it happen is one that level of confidence that I've built up over those years, failure and learning and kind of getting confident that if I keep working at it, I'm going to get there and the second thing was like creating that environment, and the team around me that supports me"

Thinking two steps ahead in your career

Athena gets bored very easily, and she uses this as a driver for thinking ahead and pursuing new challenges. As soon as things got comfortable, Athena moved on. Her moves focussed on new experiences, challenges and learning rather than merely titles or money. In the longer run, this approach has resulted in significant growth for Athena.

Using your strengths as an introvert to lead

Athena is a fantastic role model for an authentic introverted leader. From taking responsibility for organising social events to positioning speaking events as opportunities to represent her team, Athena has found her approach and motivation to scenarios that were initially uncomfortable for her. Prioritising her interactions and connecting 1:1 seem to be the way Athena maintains her energy levels.

Observations and reflections

What really stood out to me from Athena's story is the distance she manages to maintain between her job and her identity.

This helps her to put things into perspective and not get emotionally sucked into it. I believe Athena can do so by investing in herself, be it building her own brand outside work, saving up money to account for job losses, and taking charge of her career and leaving jobs when she has learned enough. She is at her career's driving seat, which, in turn, helps her maintain that healthy distance with her work. The risk of identifying with one's job is that when there is a crisis at work or if one loses their job, it makes the individual vulnerable to identity crisis, stress, anxiety and depression. All of which can be avoided by an intentional practice of creating a little distance between one's job and oneself. Ironically, distancing actually makes one better at work by freeing up emotional energy and reason to focus on work or the problem at hand rather than worrying about it. Figure 13.1 illustrates this.

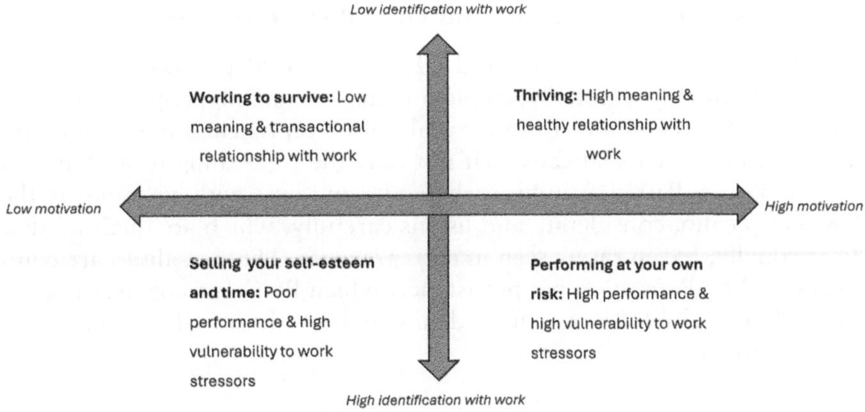

Figure 13.1 Job Identity Motivation (JIM) Matrix

Coaching questions for you

Which of the statements below resonates with you the most?

1- your job is your identity
2- your job is a significant part of your identity
3- you care deeply about your job, but it's not part of your identity
4- you care about your job, and you care about other activities outside work equally or more
5- your job is needed for paying your bills, but you couldn't care less

Reflect on your choice. Where would you like to be?

What three things you can do to shift your relationship with your job? Which one of the three can you start doing this week?

How to succeed as a calm and considerate leader

Patrick has been the founder and CEO of a social purpose-led Ed-tech scale-up with offices globally, employing more than 250 people for the last ten years. Patrick comes from a family of entrepreneurs and starting up a business with a social cause felt not only the right thing to do but also second nature. Patrick is in his early forties and lives with his family in the UK. He is calm, considerate and listens carefully, which are qualities that I, personally, haven rarely seen in entrepreneurs. These qualities are complemented by Patrick's quiet persistence, which Patrick recognises in him. "I think as a child, I would have definitely been described as persistent," recalls Patrick.

> Patrick's passion for the purpose of his business, his team and his values comes across throughout our discussion. When you talk to Patrick, you realise that this is someone who has weathered the storms that starting up a business entails and has a solid grounding and purpose to persevere and knows that he cannot do it all by himself.

Patrick started his career working as an investment manager for nearly six years. While he found this to be well-paid and dynamic, Patrick was more interested in the people and teams he met when he was assessing the businesses. He wanted to start a for-profit business with a social cause. He found an Ed tech business and later sold it to a bigger Ed-tech firm. After this, Patrick found his current business, which aims to help students from deprived backgrounds.

What kind of leader is Patrick and how does that play into how people thrive in his organisation?

Patrick believes in creating an environment of responsibility and agency and surrounding himself with smart people who can drive their functions and teams in a way that is aligned both strategically and culturally with Patrick's vision.

"It is important to create an environment of stability, commitment, trust, and agency for your team as a CEO/founder. I think I'm very good at that," says Patrick with pride.

Patrick doesn't believe in micro-management and is keen to create an environment where everyone has their space and agency and is trusted to do their job.

"If you micromanage people, they wait to be micromanaged and it's a vicious circle," says Patrick.

What kind of people thrived in your organisation, and who haven't?

Patrick explains how many of these C-level leaders grew from junior roles as graduates. The qualities that helped them grow were that they really cared about the company's purpose, were smart and competitive and really understood the importance of caring and supporting their team. Some of his external C-level hires didn't quite work out.

Tips from the CEO

So, what are your top tips for anyone looking to join a scale-up?

- Make sure you care about what the business does. This will help you navigate the highs and lows that are inevitable. It is much easier to lose hope and give up when you don't care and believe in the purpose.
- Do some research on culture by looking at Glassdoor or other relevant channels. So you've got a feeling of what you're stepping into.
- Talk to your prospective boss about their leadership style and ask questions like "What characteristics would they need to show to succeed or fail?"
- Know the maturity of the company and how that plays to your strengths. It is very different to join an early-stage start-up to joining a mature scale-up. Understanding where your skills and values are the best fit is key to success. Also, joining a company led by a young, first-time founder vs joining a company led by an experienced founder can be very different. Experience helps.

Tools

Questions to ask to your future boss during your interviews

Here is a list of questions to ask to your future boss. Of course, you can pick the ones you like and really don't have to ask all these questions. When your hiring manager answers these questions, as well as listening to the answers, please pay attention to their body language and tone, and reflect on how willingly they answer, how genuine does the answer sounds, do they give tangible examples, are they willing to accept their mistakes and learn from it, are they open to new ideas, opinions and feedback, do you feel you have some common values and skills, would this be someone you will willingly hang out for a coffee, do you sense mutual respect etc. Your intuition can guide you here.

- What builds and breaks trust with you?
- Describe your best direct report? What made them successful?
- Describe your worst direct report? What went wrong?
- What are your superpowers? What are your areas of development?
- How best to influence you?
- Where do you feel we have common skills, and where would we complement each other?
- How do you give feedback? How would you like to receive feedback?
- What is one thing I need to get right in my first 90 days?
- What does success look like in my role?
- What do you think are the key opportunities and challenges in my role? What support will be available to me?
- What steps do you take to ensure you are an inclusive leader?
- What are your key opportunities and challenges in your role? How can I help you?

Observations and reflections

As a founder of a purpose-led scale-up, Patrick's passion and personal value alignment to his business shines through. The strength that this meaningful work gives Patrick to navigate the ups and downs of the scale-up founder journey is inspiring. This also means, Patrick expects passionate employees who take ownership of part of the business and act like an owner.

Coaching questions for you

Think about your best and worst manager, what would you say are their key 3–5 values (what builds/breaks trust with them)?

____
____
____

What would you say are your key 3–5 values?

____
____
____

Identify your overlapping values and conflicting values with both of them.

___

___

___

What do you observe?

___

___

___

What can you learn from what you observe in choosing your next manager?

___

___

___

Notes

1 Chhaya, N. (2022, August 29). How to Figure Out the Power Dynamics in a New Job. Retrieved from Harvard Business Review: https://hbr.org/2022/08/how-to-figure-out-the-power-dynamics-in-a-new-job (accessed 14 Jan. 2024).
2 Wikipedia Contributors. (2019, May 8). French and Raven's Bases of Power. Wikipedia; Wikipedia Foundation. https://en.wikipedia.org/wiki/French_and_Raven%27s_bases_of_power. (accessed 15 May 2024).
3 Forsyth, D. R. (2019). *Group dynamics* (7th ed.). Cengage.
4 From Baker, T. (2015). *The New Influencing Toolkit: Capabilities for Communicating With Influence*. London: Palgrave Macmillan, 43–69.
5 Changing poison to medicine is buddhist principle called as 'hendoku-iyaku' in Japanese. This phrase is found in a passage from Nagarjuna's Treatise on the Great Perfection of Wisdom Further reading here: Changing poison into medicine. (2014, September 3). Retrieved from Tibetan Buddhist Encyclopedia: https://tibetanbuddhistencyclopedia.com/en/index.php/Changing_poison_into_medicine (accessed 15 Feb. 2024).
6 Covey, S. M. R., Merrill, R. R., & Link, G. (2012). *Smart Trust: Creating Prosperity, Energy, and Joy in a Low-Cost World*. Simon & Schuster
7 Covey, S. M. R., Merrill, R. R., & Link, G. (2012). *Smart Trust: Creating Prosperity, Energy, and Joy in a Low-Cost World.*
8 Kizilkan, K. (2024, *January 15)*. 160 Women in Tech Statistics: Challenges, Hiring Trends, and Retention. *Retrieved from Flair.hr: https://flair.hr/en/blog/women-in-tech-statistics/* (accessed 19 Feb. 2024).
9 A decade of UK tech. (2023). Retrieved from Tech Nation: https://stagetechn.wpengine.com/a-decade-of-uk-tech/#forewords

Part V

Let's focus on YOU

Chapter 14

How to thrive when you are different

Introverts, HSPs, minorities, people with ADHD or dyslexia

On one hand, scale-ups can be particularly tough environments if you are different. Due to their small size and strong culture, scale-ups can very much seem like a tribe you cannot permeate easily. Also, the lack of experience and maturity in the leadership means your differences might not be understood, which can make fitting in harder.

On the other hand, scale-ups can be the environment one might thrive with some of these differences. The lack of rigid structures and entry requirements can provide opportunities for those who are different and cannot fit in within a corporate environment.

It all depends on the context, your awareness and your approach. We will be exploring some of those differences in this chapter. This is not an exhaustive list of all the differences, but this should give you an idea of how to approach your differences and make them work for you in the context of scale-ups.

How to thrive as an introvert in scale-ups

Let's talk about introverts. This is coming from a self-confessed introvert. Over the years, I have been reading about introverts and coaching them too, so this topic is close to my heart.

There are a lot of misconceptions about being an introvert. In fact, even the Cambridge Dictionary describes introverts as

> Someone who is shy, quiet and prefers to spend time alone rather than often being with other people[1]

I recommend reading Susan Cain's international bestseller – Quiet, to understand introverts. *Shyness and introversion are not the same thing. Shyness is the fear of negative judgement, and introversion is a preference for quiet, minimally stimulating environments.*[2]

DOI: 10.4324/9781003565598-19

I prefer the description of introverts, that is, to do with where they get their energy from and where they tend to lose their energy. Understanding the brain chemistry (dopamine sensitivity and neural pathways[3]) that explains the appropriate levels of stimulation required for introverts is also key to acceptance and not trying to change oneself into an extrovert to fit in.

Being an introvert is wonderful and powerful. It is estimated that more than half of people around the world prefer introversion.[4] I will not try to explain these in detail in this book as it is an in-depth topic, but here are my key takeaway points.

- Introverts get their energy by being alone, spending time in quiet spaces, being in small groups and/or engaging in quiet activities
- Introverts get overwhelmed with too much noise, lights, clutter and too many people (lower threshold for dopamine sensitivity); hence, the right level of simulation is important for us to thrive
- Introverts have superpowers-intuition, reflection, active listening and deep thinking and many of them are highly sensitive, which means we are more tuned into our environment, people's emotions and thoughts, which can make us great influencers, coaches and leaders.
- Deep thinking and broader sensing mean our brains take longer paths so instant reaction and being put on the spot might be challenging for us. Plus, we tend to notice other people's reactions in a lot more detail, which also makes us self-conscious.

Being an introvert in a scale-up can be particularly challenging if the leadership is mostly extroverted and the culture is skewed towards favouring extroverts. This is when you see open plan design with very few quiet spaces, noisy social activities, loads of meetings and people appreciated for speaking up/presenting in front of others. Being an introvert myself, I was once asked by my scale-up manager, "You seem quite active in smaller settings but in big meetings you go quiet!" It was not a statement of observation rather something he wanted me to work on. Had I the awareness and confidence I have now, I would have responded with "Duh, that's because I am an introvert and that's something I should not have to change!" Surrounded by firefighters, introverts might be perceived as "slow" or "doesn't care enough," while all they need is more thinking time for a considered approach.

One of the founders/CEOs I worked for, was highly appreciative of my measured and considered approach, which helped me calm down and move forward when everyone around me was panicking and making flippant decisions.

So, knowing your strengths as an introvert will be valuable in the context of scale-ups, of which there are many.

Why scale-ups need you

Considered risk-taking

Introverts are naturally able to sense the warning signs and opportunities, gather multiple data and perspectives and drive the team towards a considered decision with clarity and speed. This makes you great leaders for strategic programmes that involve multiple functions, teams and ambiguity. While the rest of the team tends to jump into action and risk hasty decisions, you can be the voice of reason – helping them navigate at speed, but with considerations that will enable the business spend wisely and secure returns not just in the shortterm, but also in the long term. The extroverts will love you for this and rely on your skills. This will make you a valued and indispensable member/leader of the team. When you do this, please ensure you communicate your approach to others and share widely (in a written blog/email, perhaps) so the impact can be multiplied and that you ensure that you get the credit for your contribution.

Creative problem-solving

Introverts are creative problem solvers. When faced with complex problems, you can really shine by coming up with solutions that others haven't thought about. This makes introverts great candidates for driving new solutions and initiatives. Leverage this skill by seeking roles that involve problem-solving and creativity and share your gift with your team.

> While the rest of the team tends to jump into action and risk hasty decisions, you can be the voice of reason to help them.

Calming influence

The calm that introverts exude can be exactly the energy the team needs in moments of chaos. So, introverts can be great coaches, mentors and advisors for people who are overwhelmed by the challenges that a scale-up throws. Reach out to people when you sense they need help and add value. You will develop deeper relationships and respect by doing so. It is clearly a win-win.

What support do you need to thrive

Now, you know how you can contribute. It is equally important to know how you can be supported. Wearing your own oxygen mask first analogy works here.

Choose your role and your manager carefully

Avoid roles that require instant responses/firefighting – for example, customer service/warehouse operations or constant engagement – for example, sales (Although you might be able to shape these roles to suit your style, e.g. by building deeper relationships rather than going wider). Choose roles that involve problem-solving, creative thinking and/or longer-term planning – for example, programme management, strategy and analytics. Your ideal manager would be an extrovert who recognises your strengths and is considerate of your unique style and needs. They will amplify your contributions to the wider business while relying on your calm and considered approach. They know that you need space and intellectual stimulation. They will be your ally and your chief cheerleader. Avoid working for managers who are very much immersed in the day-to-day and don't have the vision for the longer term, are flippant and hasty in their approach or are super judgemental. While it is hard to find your ideal manager, you can sense the attributes that will work for you and those which wouldn't and choose wisely. In my experience, my ideal managers were not perfect, but they saw my strengths, were genuinely curious and open, and their weaknesses didn't block my progress. My worst managers were the exact opposite. The Myers-Briggs compatibility tests might be helpful (MBTI "NT"[5] types work well, for example), but beyond that, the most important aspect is the maturity of the individual. If you work for a mature, secure individual who can reflect on their thoughts, feelings and actions, you will enjoy the relationship and your work.

Build your allies and amplifiers

This is so important for introverts. The best way to build them is to start early. Even during the interviews, look for your allies. These are often people with whom you feel an instant rapport—you can sense their respect and genuine willingness to support you. You should build the relationship 1:1 and start understanding how you can support them, too. In this way, over a period, you will have a group of people who trust, support and value you. When things go wrong or when you are faced with a difficult decision, these are the people who will back you up and help you navigate. Ensure that some of these people are extroverts who amplify your contributions and strengths more widely. This is by far the most effective way to be recognised and build your reputation within the business.

Manage your energy

Your energy can be overused by either involving yourself in activities that don't align with your natural strength (quick drain) or by overusing your strengths (slow drain). Ensure that you plan your day to manage your energy and check in with yourself to balance it. Practices such as meditation, journaling, walking and coffee with a friendly colleague can all help you reset when you sense there is a need to pause. If the energy drain becomes a pattern, you might need to step back and ask yourself, "Am I in the right role/working with the right people/in the right way?" and do something about it to protect yourself from the risk of burnout.

Communicate your needs and preferences

Feel empowered to communicate your needs and preferences. It could be as simple as "can we have a fortnightly catch-up rather than weekly" or "do you mind if I skip the team drinks" or "could we go for lunch next time in a quieter restaurant" or "could you share with me your questions ahead." All these might seem awkward, but with practice, people get used to them- and so do you. They will make everyone's life easier and position you to succeed.

How to thrive as a highly sensitive person (HSP) in scale-ups

Many introverts are also highly sensitive like me. Extroverts can also be HSPs. It is estimated that up to one in five[6] of the world's population could be highly sensitive. HSPs, as the name suggests, are highly sensitive to their environmental stimuli and cues. We have a deep sense of appreciation for subtle things in life, be it the sights and sounds in a food market or music. We also pick up subtle emotions and sometimes come across as mind readers. This is all great, right? Yes, but this also leads to overwhelm. I suggest reading the book "The Highly Sensitive Person" by Elaine Aron to understand this trait at more depth and/or check out the HSP questionnaire that she has developed.[7]

Being an HSP is an innate trait and not a disorder. The world needs and has always needed HSPs to protect their tribe.

> If you are a highly sensitive person, you have a gift to sense subtle emotions (ever been called a "mind reader"?) and read the environment accurately ("hear sounds that others don't"?), but that also comes with a responsibility of protecting yourself from overwhelm and caring for yourself.

Carl Jung's concept of inner child[8] could be immensely useful for HSPs. Basically, in a layperson's term, we still have our younger self's (child) personality within us. The child carries those childhood wounds, fears, excitements and doubts based on early childhood experiences. The child then influences our decisions as adults. This is very relevant for us HSPs because of our sensitive nature and that means we have absorbed both good and bad more than our fellow non-HSP kids. Learning to love, care, support oneself like a parent (a concept known as re-parenting[9] in psychology) helps heal those of us who have experienced unmet needs and gaps in love, care and support from their primary carers. HSPs, unfortunately, are more likely to develop mood disorders than non-HSPs[10]. Fortunately, neuroplasticity[11] (our minds are malleable) and body/mind training such as mindfulness, yoga, sports, etc., can help address those early years' gaps and help HSPs (and many others in similar situations) live an unrestricted life. HSP's curious mind and appetite for internal reflection means they can learn how to manage the downsides of their sensitivity effectively, while leveraging the upsides.

Why scale-ups need you

You sense the opportunities and risks way before others do

Scale-ups are full of people who get stuff done (Doers), so much so, they might not be aware of what's around the corner. While businesses of that stage need more action than strategy, without a strategy, the actions can be wasted. This is where HSPs with their oracle-like sensing superpowers come in. Be it identifying patterns of problems, potential opportunities or competitive threats, HSPs can act as compasses for navigating the scale-ups to success.

You are the voice of reason and calm in chaotic times

HSPs have a calm demeanour (while on the inside, their thoughts are passing through depths and making millions of connections, and their body is sensing the subtlest signal). They don't do drama, purely for self-preservation. This can be exactly what the teams need during turbulent, uncertain times, of which there will be many, in scale-ups. HSPs can help calm the team, provide reassurance and bring back rational thinking. They can be excellent coaches and mentors for all levels of seniority. Normally, managers of HSPs find themselves getting counsel from them (if they themselves are wise and secure that is).

You have an influencing superpower

HSPs are deep listeners, astute observers of thoughts, emotional sponges and environment signal detectors, which makes them excellent influencers.

A large percentage (let's not debate how much) of communication is non-verbal. HSPs pick these signals accurately, pattern match deeply and therefore understand the thoughts, emotions and words of the speaker at a level only HSPs can. With these inputs, a well-trained HSP can influence people like no others can. Be it an idea or a project, give it to HSPs to gather engagement and momentum with the key stakeholders. This is a skill much needed in scale-ups.

> Whether your culture is awesome or awful, HSPs will sense it earlier than anyone else.

You are a culture barometer

If empowered and provided a safe space, they will tell you what's going well and what's not without sugarcoating. If you are a CEO of a scale-up, this is exactly what you need to hear. So, keep those HSPs close to you.

Now, you know how you can contribute. It is equally important to know how you can be supported.

What support do you need

You need safe spaces and safe people

Scale-ups can be vibrant and noisy environments. You need your quiet and reflective spaces. Be it a working space by the window or a meditation room, these spaces make a big difference in helping HSPs regulate their energy levels and emotions during their day. Thankfully, many scale-ups have these spaces.

The same goes with people. HSPs, more than others, need people with whom they can open up and talk freely with psychological safety. This could be their manager, a coach or simply a friendly colleague, but having someone (ideally a few) will help HSPs process their thoughts and emotions especially when they are overstimulated or overwhelmed. Although they might choose to be quiet immediately after feeling overwhelmed, they would seek help from their safe person soon after.

You need to be able to step away from the chaos

Yes, while HSPs bring calm in the storm, they can get caught up in it, and that can overwhelm them sooner than it does to others. So, it is best for HSPs, to remain on the fringes of chaos so they can help without getting drowned. In practice, this means they take the role of a coach/advisor rather than someone operating/executing during troubled times.

You need sponsorship

Everyone does, but for HSPs this is critical for success. The sponsors amplify HSP contributions and protect them from things that could overwhelm them, like office politics. This is also a door for HSPs to make an impact broader than their current role and/or seniority.

You need to operate at the right role and level

Senior strategic role yes, junior operational role no! Of course, everyone needs to start somewhere but I would say, start in a role that has a longer-term focus. Programme management, Chief of Staff, Strategy Manager, Go-to-Marketing expert, Product marketer and Analytics manager could be some roles that HSPs might thrive in, leading up to VP of Strategy, Chief Customer Officer, Chief Data Officer etc.

How to thrive as a person with ADHD in scale-ups

NHS UK website[12] defines ADHD as "a condition that affects people's behaviour. People with ADHD can seem restless, may have trouble concentrating and may act on impulse," and goes on to say

"Adults with ADHD may find they have problems with:

- organisation and time management
- following instructions
- focusing and completing tasks
- coping with stress
- feeling restless or impatient
- impulsiveness and risk-taking

Some adults may also have issues with relationships or social interaction."

These clinical descriptions, although useful in their clinical context, are often limiting and do not talk about the strengths these individuals can uniquely bring. A study conducted by Northwestern University in 2008 found that the prevalence of ADHD in nomadic tribesmen offered a distinct advantage leading to better nourishment, but the same trait was a disadvantage when found in settled men.[13]

I met a successful scale-up CPO in his forties who was diagnosed with ADHD as an adult. He feels that being in a leadership role in a scale-up environment suits his ADHD-related needs and strengths, offering the right balance of flexibility and change that helps him thrive at work. That said, he also feels that junior scale-up roles, where there maybe a lack of transparency around job security, can feel destabilising. He had worked in FTSE 100 companies at the start of his career and then transitioned to scale-ups. He feels scale-up environments are best suited for him at this stage.

I also interviewed a female scale-up leader who was diagnosed with ADHD at age eleven. She feels that the pace of change in scale-ups works in favour of her by suiting how her ADHD brain operates, and that she is "good in chaos." She feels she couldn't work in a job or environment that is static and demands routine. This means that one needs to feel comfortable with shorter tenures and that when you drive change, you are likely to make yourself redundant at some point, and that is an indicator of success.

> A scale-up environment works suits his ADHD-related needs and strength, offering the right balance of flexibility and change that helps him thrive at work.

Why scale-ups need you

Great with chaos and change

This can be a great skill while working in scale-ups. While many people might move away from chaos and dread it, people with ADHD love and thrive in it, which makes them great for driving and managing change. Exactly what scale-ups need!

Operating at speed

Scale-ups need people to move at speed. Someone with ADHD is naturally inclined to work at a faster pace and that makes them star performers in scale-ups.

Thinking out-of-the-box

When faced with big problems and limited resources (typical scale-up issue), thinking out of the box is a necessity. The ADHD brain is uniquely capable of connecting various patterns and coming up with out-of-the-box solutions.[14]

Relationship building and influencing

Navigating scale-ups requires advanced relationships and influencing skills. People with ADHD are great at that. They understand and bring multiple perspectives, sense subtle cues (almost psychic), and have strong intuition to influence. Having ADHD and managing it in difficult environments makes them more attuned to and compassionate towards other people's challenges and needs, which makes them excellent leaders in scale-ups.

Being comfortable with the lack of structure

Scale-ups lack structure and processes. You know what? That's ok for people with ADHD- that's exactly the right environment where they thrive. While people with ADHD can struggle with a structured environment and organising themselves, they are indeed great at putting in structure and organising others, which also plays to their advantage in scale-ups.

What support do you need to thrive

Individual attention

Employees with ADHD (and many other differences) have needs that require addressing. These are mostly simple adjustments that can be easily implemented with some thought and consideration and by using experts in this field. For example, sending a video to show the walk from station to office or sharing interview questions ahead of time to avoid surprises. These reasonable changes can be game-changing for someone with ADHD. It is great that we live in times when we can assert and talk about these requirements openly.

Safe people within and outside work

Everyone needs them and is better off with them, but for people with ADHD, it is pertinent that they have people both within and outside work so that they can talk openly while knowing it is safe to do so. These allies could be your friends, colleagues, partners, parents, therapists, mentors, or mindfulness teachers. It does help to have at least one safe person within work and one outside work. Especially, when dealing with overwhelming feelings or secrets, the ADHD brain can do with some channels to offload, so the anxiety bucket is managed without overflowing.

Professional support to manage anxiety/overwhelm

People with ADHD have an increased risk of anxiety.[15] It could help to seek professional help to manage anxiety. Be it medication to help maintain a calmer state, therapy or learning skills like mindfulness/yoga-finding support is key to thriving.

Awareness of concentration ebbs and flows

People with ADHD can have more ebbs and flows in their concentration than the rest of the population. It is important to work with the flow rather than against it. For example, some people find Monday evenings to be their most productive time and Fridays to be their most unproductive time, in which case, schedule your work and leisure activities accordingly - and don't feel guilty about doing so. Building self-compassion and asking for support/delegating are superpowers to embrace.

Being open about your ADHD

This one needs courage and it's okay if you are not ready or want to do so, but opening up at work can be incredibly empowering and help you find other people with similar needs. It can also help your colleagues understand you better and flex their styles to work better with you. This is a choice and one that you can experiment with slowly, starting with your safe people.

How to thrive as a person with dyslexia in scale-ups

"Dyslexia is a learning difficulty that primarily affects the skills involved in accurate and fluent word reading and spelling. Characteristic features of dyslexia are difficulties in phonological awareness, verbal memory and verbal processing speed. Dyslexia occurs across the range of intellectual abilities. It is best thought of as a continuum, not a distinct category, and there are no clear cut-off points."[16,17]

Why scale-ups need you

While there is research to suggest people with dyslexia excel at out-of-the-box thinking, I am going to simply state that people with dyslexia are simply as talented as everyone else, if not more. So, why should scale-ups need you as much as they need others? I have worked with some amazingly talented colleagues with dyslexia, and it would be a shame if they were not given equal opportunity to succeed.

What support do you need to thrive

The most challenging tasks for anyone with dyslexia at work are likely to be with reading and writing. Any environment that has rigid rules and significant reliance on one's ability to read and write effectively and quickly can be a tough environment for people with dyslexia. This also suggests that there is a lack of inclusivity by design in these environments, which in itself is a red flag.

I have worked in scale-ups, where some newly appointed leaders have brought in "word document" and "long emails" culture from bigger businesses.

In my research, while scale-ups tend to be more flexible with the communication style than bigger businesses are, this is not the case across all scale-ups. I have worked in scale-ups where some newly appointed leaders have brought in "word document" and "long emails" culture from bigger businesses. While the intent and effectiveness of these practices are good, without alternative options, they tend to exclude and/or add pressure on people with dyslexia.

So, if you are Dyslexic, what support do you need to look for in order to thrive? Choose a workplace where:

- You can talk openly about dyslexia, and/or see others do so.
- Communication options are flexible, that is, it's ok to share a word document or a PowerPoint deck or a voice mail or do a Zoom call, in most instances. Of course, some high-stakes meetings might need specific templates, but they shouldn't be the norm.
- You have a manager who can support you and push back on people picking up on pedantic with "Duh, my amazing team member is Dyslexic so please refrain from feedback on spelling/grammar" or a different version of this to fit to the context.
- You can use advanced tech tools that can simplify your life.
- You can build relationships with colleagues to help you with those high stakes written communication.

Other characteristics that make you stand out

Scale-ups can over-index on young (<30 yrs) individuals of native ethnic origin and/or those who have been educated in the local country. What this means is when you are different, you really stand out. There are both pros and cons to this, but it's not easy. I worked in one such scale-up where I was one of the very few mothers, women of colour and aged over 35. I felt like a fish out of water. What made it challenging was it was hard to integrate and find common ground especially in the social events. While I left work to pick up my daughter, the rest went to the pub for some drinks (Did I say I don't drink alcohol?). Raised in a middle-class conservative Indian family with very little exposure to adventure sports, I found the invitation to do white water rafting wearing body suits both nerve-racking and embarrassing at the same time, while my colleagues were all pumped up (at least outwardly). Over the years, I have developed skills to adapt and add value in such environments and by speaking to people who have done so.

> Don't let your difference become the elephant in the room no one asks about.

How can you integrate better?

Some of the ways people integrate when they are different are below:

Acknowledging your difference

Don't let your difference become the elephant in the room no one asks about. Embrace it and share with your colleagues (to the extent you are comfortable). I talk about my Indian origin, customs, phrases and philosophies. These have led to good laughs, creating common ground and insightful discussions. You don't want your difference to become your only identity at work but it sure is one of your identities - and you need to take pride in that. This will encourage others to respect your identity as well. I initiate celebrations of Indian festivals as a great way to acknowledge and embrace my difference and invite other people in.

Speaking up when things don't work for you

Well, how I regret not pushing back on that white-water rafting invitation (I declined it on the basis of a fear of water sports, which was also true) on the grounds that it was not inclusive! These days I push back and speak up when things don't work for me or a group of people to ensure social events are inclusive. We are talking about organising lunches, quieter group activities, office catch-ups, as well as evening parties - all to accommodate everyone's preferences and comfort levels. When you decline events, do so without guilt and ensure you communicate that you enjoy being with the team, that is, you are not rejecting spending time with the team, but the event is not suited to your preferences.

> When you decline events, do so without guilt and ensure you communicate that you enjoy being with the team.

Mentoring/coaching/offering to help

To integrate into any group, you need to add value and get value back. I think understanding the needs of the group and adding value should come first. Being different puts you in a great place to do so as you bring a different perspective. Imagine a 25-year-old living in the same country all their life vs someone with more life experience educated elsewhere and living in a vastly culturally different country. The former has a lot to learn from the latter. Don't you think so? You need to build trust and relationships, so people seek your coaching or mentorship – and that begins with opening and being vulnerable (showing you are a fellow human being who looks and speaks differently but has shared human vulnerabilities).

Bringing a different perspective

Bringing a different perspective not only helps from a coaching and mentoring point of view, it also helps in creative problem-solving and driving performance. My Indian bias for action and frugality means I help drive projects at speed and at a minimum cost. Also, having grown up in an environment with multiple personalities (11 people under one roof) and in a culture of such diversity, I have higher tolerance, patience and acceptance of differences at work. This really helps in team cohesion and inclusivity.

Being curious and sharing your view of the world

Being different means you can be more curious. I used to pretend I understood when someone mentioned a local phrase, event or show. Now, I question when I don't understand and that helps build relationships and knowledge. Also, making other people know that you don't understand local references, will help them be inclusive and/or explain things to you. Similarly, share your worldview. I say things like, there is an Indian phrase that translates to x, to help convey my point. People find it intriguing, and many folks have then followed up with that phrase and made connections to their local phrases.

What support do you need to thrive?

Diversity in leadership

I worked for a business where the leaders were all white men, six foot tall, had square jaws and private school accents. The culture was neither inclusive nor creative. Even if you find a diverse-looking and sounding leadership team, observe how the minority leaders act when they are in groups. Do they try hard to fit in (e.g. made-up accents, fake smiles and tendency to over-please), or are they their natural self as much as possible? This is a good indication of the acceptance level in the business and what it takes to succeed.

If the leaders all look and sound similar, stay away! They can call themselves "inclusive," but they never will be.

A culture that's inclusive and curious

You can sense this during your interviews. How comfortable the process and people make you feel about yourself. Say, if you are from a different country, do people talk about their experience with your country with genuine interest? For example, some companies have policies for everyone to choose which bank holidays to take a day off so they can use it for their celebratory days, which might not be Christmas or Easter. These policies are a good indication of an inclusive culture.

Mentors and sponsors

When you are different, you need mentors and sponsors more than others. Your mentors and sponsors don't have to share your differences, but they need to be aware of the challenges that come with it and be willing to support you.

A role that you can kick ass

This is important for everyone, but the stronger the value you bring to the business is, the less your differences will impact you. This means knowing your unique strength and assessing if the business needs it right now and in the future. Minorities in specialised roles, for example, engineering, data science and/or with measurable outcomes, for example, sales target, find it easier to progress in any business. If your role does not fall into that category, you can still define your unique value and ensure you are in a role that builds on your strength.

Notes

1 introvert. (n.d.). Retrieved from Cambridge dictionary: https://dictionary.cambridge.org/dictionary/english/introvert (accessed 19 Sep. 2023)
2 Cain, S. (2013). Introduction. In S. Cain, *Quiet: The Power of Introverts in a World That Can't Stop Talking*. London: Penguin.

3 Further reading: McCulloch, H. (2020, February 5). Embracing the Introverted Brain. Retrieved from Mind, Brain & Education: https://www.mindbrained.org/2020/02/embracing-the-introverted-brain/ (accessed 19 Jan. 2024).

4 Further reading: Summer, M. (2020, January 02). Introverts and Leadership - World Introvert Day. Retrieved from themyersbriggs: https://www.themyersbriggs.com/en-US/Connect-With-Us/Blog/2020/January/World-Introvert-Day-2020 (accessed 9 Mar. 2024).

5 Myers-Briggs® Overview. (n.d.). Retrieved from Myers-Briggs: https://www.myersbriggs.org/my-mbti-personality-type/myers-briggs-overview/ (accessed 1 Mar. 2024).

6 Aron, E. (1997). *The Highly Sensitive Person: How to Thrive When the World Overwhelms You.* New York: Harmony/Rodale.

7 Aron, E. (1997). *The Highly Sensitive Person: How to Thrive When the World Overwhelms You.*

8 Davis, S. (2020, July 13). The Wounded Inner Child. Retrieved from cpts foundation: https://cptsdfoundation.org/2020/07/13/the-wounded-inner-child/ (accessed 25 Apr. 2024).

9 Davis, S. (2020, July 27). Reparenting to Heal the Wounded Inner Child. Retrieved from cpts foundation: https://cptsdfoundation.org/2020/07/27/reparenting-to-heal-the-wounded-inner-child/ (accessed 17 Jan. 2024).

10 Mohammed Dosari, S. K. (2023). Prevalence of Highly Sensitive Personality and Its Relationship With Depression, and Anxiety in the Saudi General Population. *Cureus.*

11 *Neuroplasticity.* (n.d.). Retrieved from Psychology today: https://www.psychologytoday.com/gb/basics/neuroplasticity (accessed 10 Jan. 2024).

12 *Attention deficit hyperactivity disorder (ADHD).* (n.d.). Retrieved from NHS: https://www.nhs.uk/conditions/attention-deficit-hyperactivity-disorder-adhd/ (accessed 13 Jan. 2024).

13 Is ADHD An Advantage For Nomadic Tribesmen? (2008, June 10). Retrieved from Science Daily: https://www.sciencedaily.com/releases/2008/06/080609195604.htm (accessed 23 Jan. 2024).

14 White, H. (2019, March 5). *The Creativity of ADHD.* Retrieved from Scientific American: https://www.scientificamerican.com/article/the-creativity-of-adhd/ (accessed 19 Apr. 2024).

15 Ellis, R. R. (2023, September 23). *What's the Link Between Anxiety and ADHD?* Retrieved from WebMD: https://www.webmd.com/add-adhd/anxiety-adhd-link (accessed 19 Apr. 2024).

16 *About dyslexia.* (n.d.). Retrieved from British Dyslexia Association: https://www.bdadyslexia.org.uk/dyslexia/about-dyslexia/what-is-dyslexia (accessed 20 Apr. 2024).

17 Rose, J. (2009, June 19). *Identifying and Teaching Children and Young People with Dyslexia and Literacy Difficulties.* Retrieved from The Dyslexia SpLD trust: https://www.thedyslexia-spldtrust.org.uk/media/downloads/inline/the-rose-report.1294933674.pd (accessed 19 Apr. 2024).

Chapter 15

How to navigate job loss

Scale-ups generally have shorter average tenures, and that is to be expected given the changing nature and needs of the business. Having said that, not all the churns can be explained by this. Many are simply down to wrong hiring decision making and ineffective management of the new hires. So, how do you navigate these challenging situations, which are all too common in scale-ups?

How to navigate redundancies and being performed out

Redundancies and being performed out are more common in scale-ups than people might think. As a working society, we have largely lost the stigma around redundancies post-COVID, but the same thing cannot be said for being performed out. Performance-based termination can happen to even the smartest employee in a scale-up for a variety of reasons – such as being in the wrong role, working with a manager who doesn't value one's strengths, a change in strategy or simply because the pace of change means that, while you were great in the role as it was, the requirements have now shifted and you're no longer a fit – and that's fine! It is so important to realise the context when processing the shocking news of being performed out, so you can stop taking it as a personal failure.

Here is an example of such a scenario. Brigette was hired as a Director of Marketing in a scale-up. She was promised that the role would be a mix of strategy, team management and day-to-day operations. Brigette was great in the first two areas but less so in the latter. She reported to a micromanager whose strong suit was day-to-day marketing operations. Brigette felt that her manager failed to appreciate her strengths and contributions to the future scalability of the marketing team, while making a mountain out of a molehill regarding her weaker areas. This continued for a few months. The business then acquired another business. Brigette's manager spotted a marketing leader in the new company and wanted to consolidate all of group marketing under him. Although the business promised that

DOI: 10.4324/9781003565598-20

there would be no restructure following the acquisition, Brigette's manager gave her a lower rating and negotiated a package for her exit. He then made the leader from the new company the VP of Marketing. Now, is this Brigette's personal failure? Absolutely not! However, Brigette could have spotted that her hiring manager might not have been capable of recognising her strengths during her interviews (e.g. one of her interviewers commented that Brigette came across as more strategic than her manager). Brigette could have been prudent and chosen to work with someone more strategic. So, if you are finding yourself in this difficult situation (which is more common in scale-ups than you might think), ask yourself: "What can I learn from this?" instead of judging yourself as a failure. Context is everything!

Performance-based termination can happen to the smartest employee in the scale-up for a variety of reasons.

Being fired is not your fault, but it is your responsibility to learn from the experience and position yourself for success the next time.

Redundancies are also common in scale-ups. Different skills and roles are needed as the business scales, which makes reorganisation of teams a common occurrence. Fundraising and profitability challenges can put pressure on headcount leading to redundancies. Job security is not something scale-ups can offer. One needs to be prepared for this reality. Here are a few ways you can navigate this challenge:

Always ensure you are adding value in line with what you are being paid for

Don't wait for performance reviews to assess your impact – do it more often. Ask yourself: "What would not get done if I left the business tomorrow?" or "What impact am I making on the business?" Now, check if the impact is in line with your pay scale. If this is not the case, you should actively seek more opportunities to improve your impact. Impact, not workload! If you feel you are delivering more impact than expected at your current level, this may be the right time to discuss a promotion.

Position yourself and position again

When you work in a scale-up, you need to keep adjusting your role to suit the changing needs of the business. So, essentially, you are re-writing your job role and/or looking for new roles regularly. This is the only way to stay relevant in this environment. You need to keep your head above water, know where the opportunities are and seize them when you can. You snooze, you lose.

Build strong allies and nurture your network

Your internal allies are your eyes and ears. They will tell you what's going on, helping you position yourself. They will also put you up for new opportunities. So, invest in them. The same applies to your external network. When your boat gets rocky, your external network can be your lifeboat, so it is important to nurture them. Stay in touch with them and help them as much as you can – you never know when you will need them.

Know your skill and build your brand

You need to know your USP (unique selling point) and talk about it in your professional circle (e.g. LinkedIn or external events/networks). This will help you build a brand outside your business, supporting your career moves and winning the respect of your colleagues. When you know you can stand on your own two feet, the wave of changes in your business will affect you far less.

Have options to replace your paycheque

I can't stress how important this is. Build that financial safety net and know how you can find work at short notice, for example, freelancing – so you don't feel stressed about making ends meet in the event of losing your job. Having this also means you can take your time to find your next role and set yourself up for success. Many people fall into the same hole repeatedly because of the rush to earn the next month's paycheque. If you can extricate yourself from that pressure, it will take you a long way. I have seen even successful senior folks struggle after losing their job due to tight finances.

How to navigate when you decide to move on

Scale-ups can make you question whether you should quit more often than if you work in a larger company. Usually, you get to this point either because a change has made your working life unpleasant to unbearable, or because your hope that things will improve has been lost. Either way, your question is an important one to address. The question of "When to grit vs when to quit"[1] requires reflection, consideration and timely action. When you look closely at the situation (usually with the help of a coach, a mentor, or an ally), you will begin to recognise patterns. The key question to ask yourself is: "Are these patterns for me to address?" or "Are these patterns external to me and out of my control?." If the answer is the former, you need to address that first before making any decision, but if it is the latter, that will require further thought.

While there is no one-size-fits-all solution for every situation, here are some principles you can follow to help you make your decision.

Take time to pause

This is so important – and so difficult - as we all feel the urge to find another job as soon as possible. Under stress, your amygdala takes charge and cuts off the access to your rational brain. Guess what? Your decisions become irrational. So, taking time to engage in restful activities resets your brain from stress, resulting in a state where you are set up to make your best decisions. I sometimes used to wonder how people manage to take holidays after a job loss while I would be applying for jobs feverishly. Now, I understand the wisdom of taking a break in times of crisis.

Get a coach

In times of dilemma and transition, coaching can be invaluable and save you considerable cost and pain down the line. A great coach will help you move forward with clarity, using your own insights and values. They will help you identify your own biases and limiting thoughts, and bring a broader perspective to your situation – all of which will help you untangle yourself and make progress. In hindsight, I really wish I had engaged a coach for every job move and transition. I certainly am doing so now and will continue to do so going forward. It's a gift.

In times of dilemma and transition, coaching can be invaluable and save you considerable cost and pain down the line. A great coach will help you move forward with clarity, using your own insights and values.

Think long term

While the situation you are facing might be all-consuming at the moment, it is really important to zoom out and think long term. Ask yourself: What type of role plays to my strengths now and in the future? How long do I see myself working? What kind of culture aligns with my values? These questions will help you make decisions not just for the next year, but for a decade or more.

Be honest about your internal patterns

Sometimes, the reason you feel unfulfilled, demotivated or undermined repeatedly in a job could be down to your own patterns. You might have some limiting beliefs standing in your way, or perhaps you are simply not suited to the role and/or the environment. It is important to seek clarity on this as soon as you feel the slightest hunch. Doing so can help you save a lot of pain down the line. I highly recommend seeking support from a professional coach, therapist, or mentor to help you gain self-awareness – the first step in committing to your self-growth.

Recognise when to grit and when to quit

With all the best will in the world, you cannot change everything. If you find yourself in an incompatible or toxic environment, you need to recognise that it's time to move on. Grit often is overrated. The best approach is to discern when to grit - and when it's wiser to quit. Quitting is brave too. Hold your head high and decide to move on if needed.

> Saying, this isn't for me, is a big point of personal growth
> (Burn-out coach for professionals)

If you are making this decision right now, here are some tips:

Prioritise your wellbeing above everything else

No job or relationship in this world is worth damaging your mental health. Becoming clinically depressed, for example, can take months to recover from – and sometimes years of reprogramming efforts to develop a helpful mindset. While this can lead to a profound self-growth path, it is not something I wish upon anyone, especially when it can be prevented.

No job or relationship in this world is worth damaging your mental health.

Work out your options and decide

You can easily become quite narrow-minded when under stress, but it is important to look wider and work out your options and timing carefully. This way, you can quit when it is right for you - and with options to work through.

Get inputs but reduce the noise around your decision

It can be invaluable to seek inputs from your friends, family, mentors and colleagues. However, once you have received the inputs needed, it is important to reduce the noise around your decision. Take some time off to think (or not think) about your situation – ideally in a different environment, such as on holiday, at a retreat, or while engaging in physical activity - and decide with a clear mind.

Note

1 David, S. (2024, June 16). *The Hidden Benefits of Quitting*. Retrieved from Susan David: https://www.susandavid.com/newsletter/when-to-grit-and-when-to-quit/ (accessed 28 Jun. 2024)

Chapter 16

How to navigate a mental health breakdown

Prevention is better than cure, but unfortunately, many of us will find ourselves in a position where our mental health has already taken a toll. perhaps and you are facing burnout, anxiety or depression – all of which can impact your ability to cope, let alone perform at work. Early detection can be helpful, so be aware of the signs and be honest when you do your self-assessment. Seek support as soon as possible. You can start by opening up to a family member or a friend and by seeing your General Practioner (GP). If you have an official diagnosis of a mental health condition from your GP, how should you navigate this at work? I am sharing my experience and knowledge here, so please note that this is not official medical or legal advice.

Someone who is undergoing mental health challenges is probably also questioning themselves constantly, which makes it harder to assert themselves at work.

Opening up about mental health at work is still very hard, although we, as a society, have come a very long way in the last decade, especially post-COVID. Most people now understand what mental health is and the common issues people face. However, unless someone has experienced significant[1] mental health issues themselves or is trained in the subject, it is still not something people can easily understand or relate to. There is also uncertainty and shame associated with it –, infact it is more straightforward to open up about surgery and share clear timelines for recovery than to open up about clinical depression, where recovery timelines are often unknown. Someone who is undergoing mental health challenges is probably also questioning themselves constantly, which makes it harder to assert themselves at work. I understand this, having experienced anxiety and depression myself at one point in my life and subsequently supporting and coaching people facing similar challenges.

DOI: 10.4324/9781003565598-21

Here are my learnings

Open up to at least one safe person at work about your experience

In my case, it was my manager who fortunately (for me) had experienced anxiety himself. I can't be grateful enough for his support back then. He went above and beyond, giving me hope and encouragement when I needed it most. Together, we worked on a plan to define my role with clear boundaries, arrange some time off and organise a phased return to work. He also challenged me when I needed it. Not everyone will be lucky to find a manager like that, but I am sure you can find at least one person at work with whom you can be open about your experiences and gain some clarity in those difficult times.

Share to the extent you are comfortable with

As much as I advocate opening up about mental health, I have also experienced judgement when I opened up to the wrong people or when I was not ready. So, use your discretion and be open to the extent needed, and only with the people you feel safe with. For some, this might be saying they need a few months off for personal reasons - and that's fine. For others, it might mean sharing a LinkedIn post detailing their mental health challenges and the medication they are taking – which is also fine. Do what's best for you. There is no one-size-fits-all approach.

Understand and share your needs

Know your rights.[2] Ask yourself what your need is right now when it comes to work. For me, work helped me focus on something positive, but I needed some flexibility to work from home and take some hours off during the day. So, I took on a project which I could work on quite independently and manage my own hours. For others, it might mean taking a few months off, or maybe no change at all. Listen to your body and mind, decide what you need and then communicate it to your manager so you can work on a joint plan. Remember, you are in no different a situation from someone with a physical illness, such as cancer, so there is absolutely no shame in discussing your needs.

Avoid making big decisions

This is a big one. I sold many of my valuable shares because of my mindset during challenging times. The world appeared hopeless to me which was obviously a symptom of what I was experiencing. That was a mistake. Please do not make such mistakes when you are going through something similar. Take a leap of faith—even if you can't feel it—and let those big, future-oriented decisions wait. If a decision can't wait, use someone else's decision-making capacity to help guide you.

Give yourself time and permission to heal

When I was going through anxiety and depression, I used to feel accountable for reporting my progress to my family and manager - until one day, my friend asked me, "Why are you reporting your progress to me? You are not accountable to anyone. Just relax." It dawned on me - that's right. I don't need to recover in a certain time. I can take the pressure off and let the natural process work itself through. And it did. Health issues are a leveller. You can't, and shouldn't, try to project- manage them (no matter how good a project manager you are 😊). It only makes it worse, like ripping off a bandage repeatedly to check on a wound. Let the healing happen. It is an invaluable phase to relax, reflect and connect with yourself. You will look back at these times as periods of incredible personal growth. If you are interested in a reading list, (and please don't overdo reading, as I did) please refer to the further reading section.[3]

Notes

1 When I say significant, I mean, something that has disrupted one's life and has caused them to change their lifestyle for a certain period.

2 Supporting mental health at work Mental health and the law. (n.d.). Retrieved from acas: https://www.acas.org.uk/supporting-mental-health-workplace (accessed 19 May 2024)

3 Further reading:

Chodran, P. (2002). *When Things Fall Apart: Heart Advice for Difficult Times*. Boston: Shambhala Pubns.

Dennis Greenberger, C. A. (2015). *Mind Over Mood, Second Edition: Change How You Feel by Changing the Way You Think*. New York: Guilford Press.

Jeffers, S. (2007). *Feel the Fear and Do it Anyway*. London: Random House.

Halliwell, E. (2016). *Into the Heart of Mindfulness: Finding a Way of Well-being*. Piatkus.

Schwartz, R. (2023). *No Bad Parts: Healing Trauma & Restoring Wholeness with the Internal Family Systems Model*. Vermilion.

The Dalai Lama, H. C. (1999). *The Art of Happiness: A Handbook for Living*. Hodder Paperbacks.

Crawford, J. (2017). *Anxiety Relief: Self Help (With Heart) For Anxiety, Panic Attacks, And Stress Management*. CreateSpace Independent Publishing Platform.

Chapter 17

How to re(build) your emotional capacity

One of the key learnings for me, based on my own experience and from the patterns that I observe in successful scale-up leaders, is that there is a need for significant emotional capacity to thrive in such an environment. A large part of this is a growth mindset and practices that help sustain emotional capacity during tough times. With the right motivation, support, time and effort, everyone can build significant emotional capacity.

> While some may be fortunate to have had experiences and a genetic makeup to make them less vulnerable to breakdowns, thanks to neuroplasticity and mind-body connection, we can all actively build this key resource within ourselves.

So, there is reason for hope - indeed, excitement.

The first thing to know is the emotional capacity needed to thrive in your work is mostly built outside your work. Here are some of the ways you can build emotional capacity, and I am going to elaborate on one of them – coaching, mentoring, finding sponsors, building a network outside work, physical movement, travelling and connecting with nature.

And there is mindfulness.

Mindfulness: The most powerful skill I have personally learnt and continue to practise and learn is mindfulness. Many leadership experts are now leaning into mindfulness as the primary leadership skill, that is, leading oneself first before leading others.

> If you can't lead your whole self - thoughts, emotions, sensations, urges - how can you lead others? Mindfulness helps you learn and practise this life-enhancing skill.

DOI: 10.4324/9781003565598-22

There has been a lot of research and buzz around mindfulness in recent years, but as a wise person once said to me, "Eating in a restaurant is not the same as reading the menu." Some people think of mindfulness as simply being present in the moment and assume this is something that doesn't need training and practice. That's not true in my own experience. As simple as it sounds, it is not easy and requires skilful teachers to learn from.

I came to mindfulness in a desperate attempt to escape my anxiety and depression. One of my friends recommended the best-seller "Mindfulness: A Practical Guide to Finding Peace in a Frantic World" by Mark Williams and Dr. Danny Penman.[1] I listened to the audiobook and tried a few practices. It gave me a sense of calm, but I didn't quite unleash the superpower of mindfulness until I was recommended a teacher to learn from about a year later. I signed up for an eight-week online MBSR (Mindfulness-Based Stress Reduction) course, which was developed by Jon Kabat-Zinn in the 1970s, after he successfully helped patients with terminal and chronic illness using a secular form of Buddhist mindfulness practice in his clinic at Massachusetts Medical School.[2]

I want to clear a couple of myths about mindfulness that I hear over and over again from many people and share what I learnt from my experience. I am not claiming to be an expert on this so caveating this.

- Mindfulness is a way of life. Meditation is a big part of it, but mindfulness is also about how you relate to life outside the meditation practice through a skilful mindset.
- Mindfulness meditation is not about achieving a thoughtless state. It is a practice of observing your thoughts, emotions and sensations with loving kindness and curiosity, and without judgement, and returning your attention gently back to something you want to focus on. The thoughts, emotions and sensations are not distractions to the practice. The process of noticing and bringing the attention back is the practice! So, one can't go wrong with it. Meditation is like running on a treadmill each day to build your muscle memory for a potential marathon.
- Everyone can meditate! And with practice reap the benefits meditation offers in their day-to-day life.

It might be that I came to mindfulness at a time I had the most need, but I found the sessions fascinating. It was like an experiment to understand my mind. The practices might sound silly to the untrained – scanning your body and noticing those tingling sensations or tasting a raisin with so much awareness that it feels like you are eating the raisin for the first time in your life. I knew this was something! I continue to be fascinated as I enter my fifth year of having "found" mindfulness. Mindfulness has helped me become more aware, manage my attention, emotions and thoughts better, become more compassionate with myself and others, seek challenges with curiosity and generally be more courageous and flexible in my life. The thing to note about mindfulness though is that it is a lifelong practice. Our minds quite easily and naturally go back to our default tendencies without constant practice. So, I fully recommend mindfulness, and I wish you luck on the life-long journey.

If you are still not convinced, there are several research findings to prove that practising meditation can change your brain structurally to improve empathy, compassion and response to stress.[3]

If you want to learn mindfulness, there are some links for you to check out.[4,5]

Notes

1 Williams, M., & Penman, D. (2011). *Mindfulness*. Hachette UK.
2 If you are interested in learning about the origins of Jon Kabat-Zinn's work, there are plenty of interviews, documentary and practices on Youtube
3 *Catapult Your Leadership Now: Why Mindfulness Is The Mother Of All Leadership Skills*. (2020, August 10). Retrieved from Forbes: https://www.forbes.com/sites/ellevate/2020/08/10/catapult-your-leadership-now-why-mindfulness-is-the-mother-of-all-leadership-skills/?sh=4595c2a4b4ba (accessed 26 Sep. 2023)
4 *Choose an event or course*. (n.d.). Retrieved from Oxford Mindfulness: https://courses.oxfordmindfulness.org/learn-categories/ (accessed 28 Sep. 2023)
5 *One-to-One Mindfulness Coaching/Mentoring*. (n.d.). Retrieved from Mindfulness Sussex: https://mindfulnesssussex.co.uk/ (accessed 28 Sep. 2023)

Part VI

Conclusion

Chapter 18

How to turn your insights into practice

"I thought being smart and great at my job was all that I needed to succeed in a scale-up, but I was wrong - and I learnt it the hard way. How I wish this book had existed when I transitioned to scale-ups!" was the comment from one of my beta readers. This perfectly summarises why I wrote this book. I wanted to provide a timely and handy toolkit for anyone who wants to thrive - or help others thrive in - scale-ups. This is exactly what you should feel you have if you have reached this point.

In Part III, we discussed what to look for when interviewing and how to navigate your first 90 days. We also looked at the common toxic patterns in scale-ups and how to manage these.

The key takeaway is to really do your due diligence during the hiring process and focus on understanding the dynamics and building trust with your colleagues in your first months, as it will set you up for success. Beware of the urge to prove at the cost of learning or building relationships.

In Part IV, we learnt from real-life stories of scale-up leaders who had experienced both struggling and thriving.

Not making your job your identity and building exceptional influencing skills stood out from these stories – along with other valuable learnings.

In Part V, we focussed on you - how you can thrive if you are different or faced with difficult situations at work or with your mental health, and how you can build your emotional capacity with powerful practices.

You have unique strengths to add value, and unique needs that require support. Understanding these can be your superpower.

In each of the chapters, you learnt from stories, explored frameworks and tools, and worked through coaching questions and exercises.

Now, how do you apply all that you have learnt in real life

Having awareness of challenges and knowledge on how to manage them is a great first step, but that alone will not help you manage such situations

DOI: 10.4324/9781003565598-24

in your real life. To master these skills and find your own way of applying them, you need practice and continuous learning.

Before you dive in though, are you 100% sure that scale-ups are the ideal environment for you to thrive?

If your answer is "no," – that is absolutely fine – you should make the change before it is too late. Quitting scale-ups doesn't make you a failure in this case. Instead, saying "this is not for me" could be the wisest thing you do, setting you up for years of fulfilment, ease and satisfaction.

If your answer is "not sure," that is absolutely fine too. You have some work to be done to understand your ideal environment. Perhaps, this will come up with experience if you are early in your career, or you could get some career coaching to help you answer this question.

I hope for most of the readers, the answer will be "yes." For you, my friends, Figure 18.1 is a scale-up emotional superpower practice framework.

You can remember this practice with the abbreviation TOSTRI (Latin for Toaster).

Know Thyself

Self-awareness is the first step towards developing emotional intelligence. How well do you know yourself? If you can answer the questions below in less than three minutes, I would say, you have a good understanding of yourself. If not, there is work to be done.

- List your 3–5 values, for example, respect, productivity, independence and financial security
- List your superpower at work, for example, I connect multiple stakeholders and steer them towards a common goal with clarity
- What do you need at work to be successful? For example, inclusive environment, quiet time, supportive manager, empowerment.

Understand Others

When you have a lot to get done, there is a tendency to skip the small talk - but how can you get things done without getting a sense of what others are thinking and feeling? For example, you can push all you want, but if your colleague is worried about their partner who is waiting for a health diagnosis, they are going to be distracted. I would rather know that and acknowledge it, so we can set realistic expectations and build a supportive relationship for the future.

That's why the beginning and end of the meetings and water cooler conversations, are so powerful. In the world of hybrid working, weekly check-ins can help achieve the same effect.

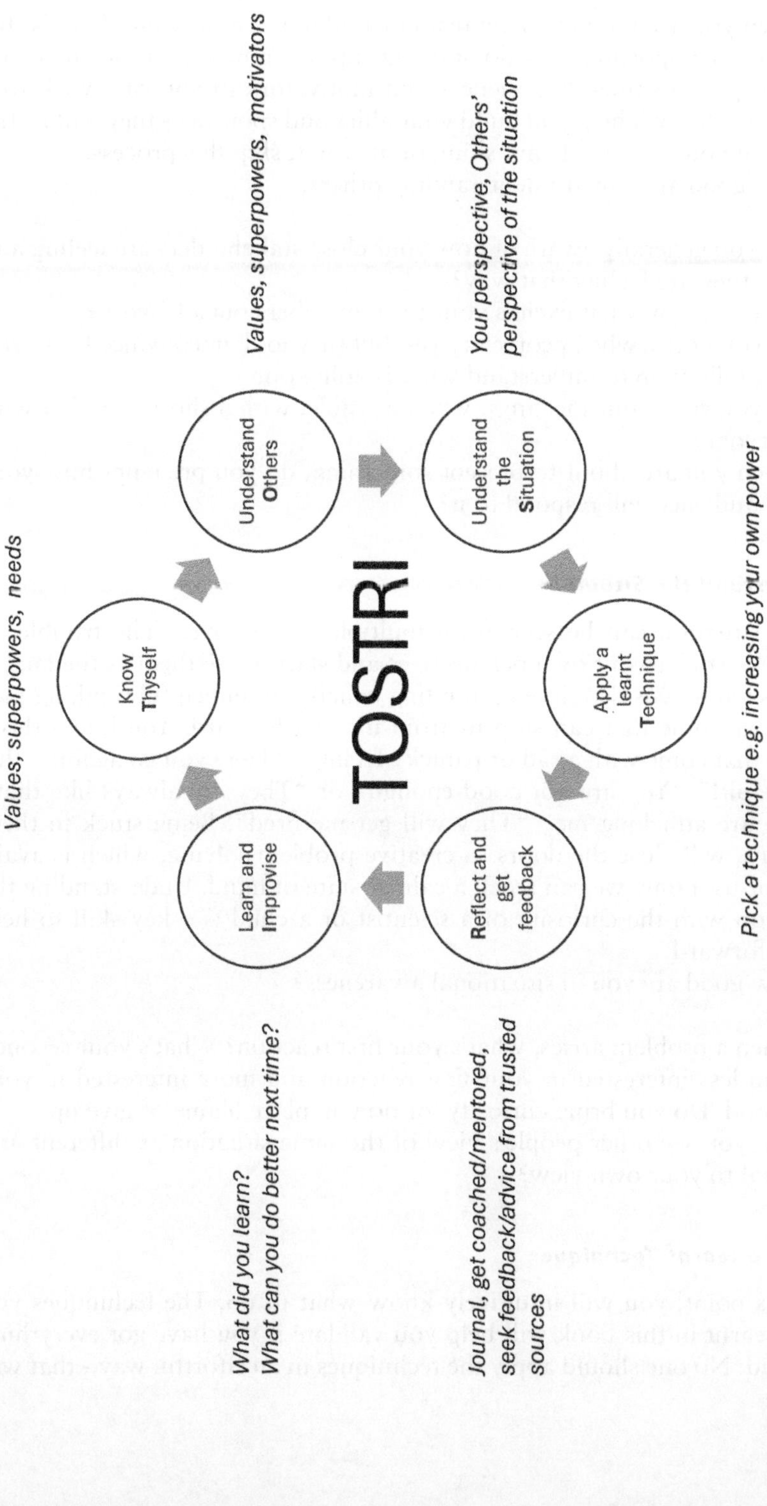

Figure 18.1 Emotional Superpower Practice Framework TOSTRI

When you are joining a new team or building a new team, there is this window of opportunity to do some group awareness exercises to really dive deep into values, experiences and motivators so you can work well together. This will help you build your allies and sponsors - they will be the pillars of your success. Don't skim, or at worst, skip this process.

How good are you at understanding others?

- Are you generally aware of how your close stakeholders are feeling and why they are feeling that way?
- Do you know what excites your team members outside work?
- Do you notice when people say yes, but they look unconvinced? Do you then follow up to understand what is going on?
- Do you start your meetings, when possible, with a short chit-chat with everyone?
- When you are about to present something, do you pre-empt how your key audience will respond to it?

Understand the Situation

Every situation can be seen from multiple perspectives. The trouble is, when we stick to our own perspectives and start to see them as the fact, it gets us stuck. We also develop limiting beliefs and unhelpful thinking patterns over time that can stop us from moving forward. You know those voices that come with a sad or panicky feeling - "Here you go again!" "It's your fault!" "You are not good enough" or "They are always like that" "They are attacking me" "They will get me fired". Being stuck in these patterns, will close the doors to creative problem-solving, which is available for us if only we can reach a calmer state of mind. Understanding the situation with the curiosity of a scientist or a child is a key skill to help move forward.

How good are you in situational awareness?

- When a problem arises, what's your first reaction? What's your second?
- I am less interested in your first reaction and more interested in your second. Do you bring curiosity, or do you place blame or give up?
- Can you see other people's view of the same situation as different and equal to your own view?

Apply a learnt Technique

At this point, you will intuitively know what to do. The techniques you have learnt in this book will help you validate if you have got everything covered. No one should apply the techniques in an effortful way - that will not be effective to say the least. The techniques are there for a reason and they work, but they work best when you apply them in your own way and back them with your own intuition.

- Pick one of the skills/techniques from this book that you would like to practise.
- How will you modify it to make it your own?
- What would be your intuitive approach if you didn't know this technique?

Reflect and get feedback

Reflecting is getting feedback from yourself. This is a powerful practice. All you need is some time, a quiet space and an intention. You can write down your reflections in a journal or reflect with a coach, a mentor or a friend. It is important for the other person to be able to provide you with a safe, non-intrusive and supportive space so you can think, feel, sense and put words to your internal happenings. You will be surprised at what you find through this process.

> Feedback from others is a gift. Unfortunately, feedback has become synonymous with "negative" comments. It shouldn't be negative at all. When you get feedback with compassion, care and candour, it truly is a gift.

While you cannot control what feedback is given to you and how, you can certainly choose people whom you can ask for feedback and share with them how you would like to receive it, for example, Can you give me an example of the impact of my action on you? Adam Grant, in his book "Hidden Potential" calls this "mining for gold,"[1] - that is, getting feedback from people who care about you, have credibility and knows you well.

Here are some questions to reflect on this topic:

- How often do you set aside time to reflect in a week?
- How often do you seek feedback?
- In the last 3 months, have you changed any of your actions based on either your reflections or feedback?

Learn and Improvise

Learning from your successes and failures, and that of others, and improvising for the next time, is key to continuous learning. This is something performers in sports, art, music and drama know very well. The same applies to our behaviours when we want to transform them one step at a time. My friend recently wrote a book titled "Do Sweat the Small Stuff,"[2] which is all about micro-interactions and how it all adds up to build your credibility as a leader.

- Think of the last time you learnt a new skill. What helped you improve continuously?
- Now, how can you apply the same process to small changes in your behaviours at work?
- What mindset can you bring to make this process effective and enjoyable?

But where is the time in my busy schedule to develop such a practice? I hear you!

Well, the trick is to embed this in your weekly rhythm, so it doesn't become another big thing to do.

In fact, some of these steps are one-offs that you can do when you join a new team, for example, sharing your values and learning about others' values. You will be surprised how these exercises can help you connect with your colleagues in a deeper way in a short time.

If you can book some time for reflection in your calendar - say one hour on a Friday - when you can reflect and learn from your experiences in that week, it can be really valuable and will make you build a habit.

Can you do this by yourself, or do you need

I strongly believe your emotional capacity improves when you connect and seek help. It might be in a formal setting with an expert such as a coach or a therapist, or in an informal setting with a mentor or a colleague - but your human skills need human involvement.

As with any skill, you're learning starts with an awkward over-effort and ends with flawless ease. So, brace yourself and be kind with yourself while you practise.

You are guaranteed success! Here is why.

When you start knowing yourself better, you put your best foot to others - and that helps you connect and understand others better. With the help of your connections, you get a clearer view of the problems and challenges, and together you can work towards solving them. With your curious and open mind, you improve your approaches and that develops stronger relationships. This is a virtuous cycle you can create, simply by taking the first step.

The alternative is blaming, feeling guilty, feeling like a failure, running away and falling into the same holes. I know which option I would choose for myself.

I want to finish off this book with a few closing words of wisdom gained from my own experience and all the people I have spoken to on this topic:

- Smarts will get you a great job in a scale-up, but it will not be enough for you to succeed.
- To succeed in scale-ups, you need to seek change and thrive in chaos - it is not enough just to tolerate them.
- If you haven't learnt the process of failing often and learning from your mistakes, scale-ups are not yet your place to be.
- Influencing a broad range of people is one of the key skills you need to master to thrive in the world of scale-ups – much more so than in larger companies.
- When you face problems, don't be quick to judge yourself or others. Most problems arise due to a combination of dynamics and situations – and most can be addressed.
- Know when to grit and when to quit. Both are courageous decisions when taken with the right intention.
- You can't take anything for granted in scale-ups, so brace yourself for a bumpy ride.
- Develop a little distance from your work and choose not to make your work your identity. In the chaotic world of scale-ups, you can get a sense of ground beneath your feet through the other parts of your life, and if you are one of the enlightened ones, develop the skill to be comfortable with groundlessness.

Thanks again for reading this book so far. Scale-ups are truly unique places for significant personal and professional growth and excitement. I hope this book helps you thrive and surf the waves with a bit more ease and confidence.

Notes

1 Grant, A. (2023). In A. Grant, *Hidden Potential: The Science of Achieving Greater Things* (p. 57). London: WH Allen.

2 Langslow, S. (2024). *Do Sweat the Small Stuff: Harness the power of micro-interactions to transform your leadership*. Northwich: Practical Inspiration Publishing.

Reference

Able, V. (2020, June 8). The Ground is Always Shifting - Pema Chodron. The Dewdrop. https://thedewdrop.org/2020/06/08/the-ground-is-always-shifting-pema-chodron/

Index

Note: *Italicized* and **bold** page numbers refer to figures and tables respectively.

For Product Safety Concerns and Information please contact our EU
representative GPSR@taylorandfrancis.com Taylor & Francis Verlag GmbH,
Kaufingerstraße 24, 80331 München, Germany

Printed and bound by CPI Group (UK) Ltd, Croydon, CR0 4YY
08/10/2025
01971992-0002